CLOCKS IN COLOR

Clocks in Color

ANDREW NICHOLLS

Photography Bob Loosemore

Macmillan Publishing Co., Inc.
New York

Macmillan Publishing Co., Inc.
866 Third Avenue, New York, N.Y. 10022

Library of Congress Cataloging in Publication Data

Nicholls, Andrew.
　Clocks in color.

　(Macmillan color series)
　Bibliography: p.
　Includes index.
　1. Clocks and watches. I. Title.
NK7484.N53　1976　　681´.13　　75-17890.
ISBN 0-02-589460-9

First American Edition 1976

Color printed by Colour Reproductions, Billericay
Text printed and books bound in Great Britain by Tinling Ltd, Merseyside

Contents

I

Early History

The wheel, the steam engine and the aeroplane have each transformed life in their turn, but perhaps the clock affects our daily lives more than any other invention. The measurement and subdivision of time have very ancient roots in the science of astronomy. By observing the apparent movements of the sun and moon, men arrived at a system in which the year is divided into days and months. In the Middle Ages European life was based upon agriculture and controlled by the seasons. Ancient manuscripts show that events could only be recorded as occurring at, for example, dawn or mid-day, since no precise time could be given.

The monasteries, which were the centres of learning, had their days divided into the seven canonical hours of Matins, Lauds, Prime, Terce, Sext, None and Vespers. At these times a bell was tolled to call the monks to prayer. The only way of knowing the time was by unreliable time-candles, waterclocks and sandglasses, all of which would be checked against the sun dial. Since the monasteries urgently needed an improved timekeeper, it seems probable that the mechanical clock was invented by monks, and indeed may have been developed independently in several different countries.

Certainly by 1300, the new invention was known in most European countries, and many clocks were constructed in public places so that the whole community could regulate its day. At first these clocks had no dials and simply struck the hours on a large bell, the period of day and night now being divided into twenty-four equal hours. The provision of a dial to mark the time was a small step forward and

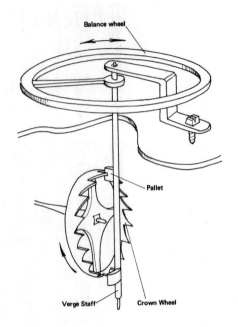

Balance wheel

Pallet

I. VERGE ESCAPEMENT
CONTROLLED BY BALANCE
WHEEL

Verge Staff   Crown Wheel

only required a simple arrangement of wheels to drive the hand or hands from the main mechanism. But, even as late as the eighteenth century, turret clocks were made with no dial and so many village church clocks still only struck the hours.

The clock was by no means the first instrument to function by means of cogs or toothed wheels. For example, the machinery of windmills and watermills is very similar, but instead of using the power of wind or water, the clock uses the constant force of a weight to turn its wheels.

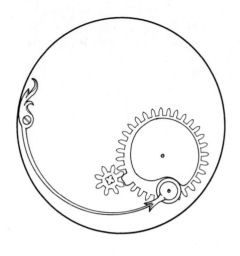

The Verge Escapement

Any mechanical clock requires some device to regulate the speed at which the wheels rotate. This is known as an escapement, since it allows one tooth of a wheel to escape at each swing of the regulator, which is usually a balance of some form or a pendulum. The first form of escapement was the verge, and it was universally employed until about 1670. In the early weight-driven clocks the part of the escapement which actually controlled the clock's speed was the foliot (plate 1). This consisted simply of a horizontal bar, with adjustable weights on the ends, mounted on the verge staff. The further from the centre of oscillation they were placed, the slower the foliot would swing. Another early form of regulator was the balance wheel (fig. 1). Unlike the foliot it had no form of adjustment, so that the only way to make fine changes in the rate of the clock was to add or subtract small weights from the driving weight.

The Spring-Driven Clock

Even the smallest weight-driven clocks were not portable and could not conveniently be moved from one room to another. The coiled

9

spring-driven clock solved this problem and gave rise to the table clock. Recent research indicates that the coiled spring was being used in the early fifteenth century on the continent of Europe. The production of the spring itself was most difficult. There would be many failures before a reliable spring was made.

An immediate drawback of the coiled spring is that it exerts a greater force when fully coiled than when it is nearly run down. To equalise the force the early German makers sometimes used a device known as stackfreed (fig. 2). A strong spring, carrying at its end a small roller, presses against a shaped cam mounted on a toothed

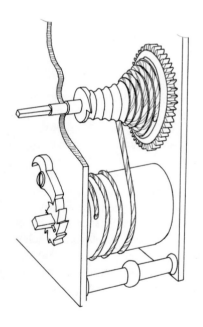

3. FUSÉE CONNECTED TO SPRING BARREL BY A GUT LINE

wheel not fully cut. A pinion on the mainspring arbor strikes the stop on the wheel after only a few turns, thus preventing overwinding and ensuring that only the turns of the spring which are nearly equal in force are used. As the mainspring unwinds so the shaped cam revolves and the friction caused by the little roller decreases. The stackfreed, however, was inefficient and little used.

The fusée was a much simpler and more effective device in use by the mid-fifteenth century. In medieval Latin *fusata* meant a spindle full of thread which the fusée resembled (fig. 3). The principle of the fusée is that of the lever. When the spring is fully coiled and the gut is all wound onto the cone-shaped fusée, the pull from the spring acts upon the smallest diameter. As the spring unwinds, the extra leverage of the increased diameter of the fusée equalises the force transmitted to the train of wheels.

The Pendulum

Although great advances had been made, until the mid-seventeenth century few clocks could keep time to within a quarter of an hour a day. The use of a pendulum to regulate a clock changed this. Both Leonardo da Vinci and Galileo are known to have realised the possibility of controlling clockwork with a pendulum, and it is believed that Galileo partially constructed a pendulum clock but died before it was completed. The Campani brothers of Rome also experimented with pendulum clocks in the 1650s, but it was the Dutch scientist, Christian Huygens, who put the principle into practical use in 1657. Very soon the pendulum clock was widely adopted in Europe (fig. 4).

The advantage of the pendulum was that it was isochronous – that is, its swing was always equal and depended only on its length. Neither its own weight, nor the angle of arc through which it swung, altered the time that each swing took. Within six months of the introduction of the pendulum, clocks could be made to keep time to within a minute or two a day. This made it practical to fit a minute- as well as an hour-hand, although this was not a universal practice.

During the next fifteen years, under the patronage of Charles II, English makers invented a new escapement, the anchor, for use with

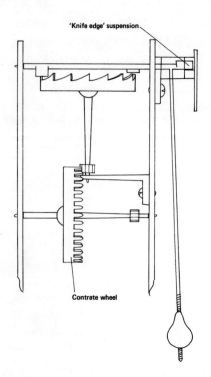

'Knife edge' suspension

Contrate wheel

4. VERGE ESCAPEMENT AND BOB PENDULUM

a long pendulum (fig. 5). Although it is thought to have been Dr Robert Hooke who realised the added advantage of the long pendulum, both he and the clockmakers, William Clement and Joseph Knibb, have a claim to the invention of the anchor escapement.

By the early eighteenth century it was realised that the recoil of the anchor escapement produced too much friction, thus interfering with the pendulum's swing and reducing the clock's accuracy. Around 1715 George Graham, Thomas Tompion's successor, invented a dead beat escapement (fig. 6). The drawing shows how the pallet has two faces instead of the single curved one of the anchor. When

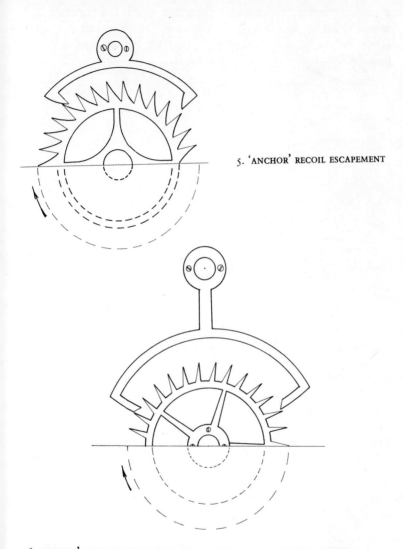

5. 'ANCHOR' RECOIL ESCAPEMENT

6. GRAHAM'S DEAD BEAT ESCAPEMENT INVENTED IN THE EARLY EIGHTEENTH CENTURY

a tooth is released it falls onto a locking face which does not cause the wheel to recoil, since the face is part of an arc centred at the pallet arbor. As the pendulum returns, the tooth gives the pendulum an impulse as it moves down the impulse face.

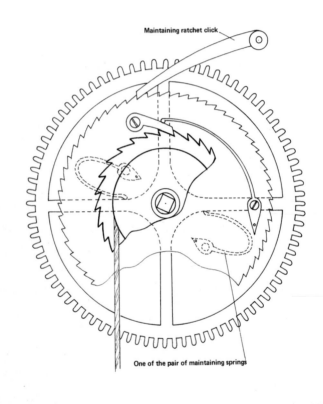

Maintaining ratchet click

One of the pair of maintaining springs

7. HARRISON'S MAINTAINING POWER DEVICE WHICH SUPERSEDED THE BOLT AND SHUTTER FORM OF MAINTAINING POWER IN THE EARLY EIGHTEENTH CENTURY

Maintaining Power

When a clock is being wound and the motive power is removed, it is possible for the clock to stop or the escape wheel may even trip backwards. As well as losing time it is also possible for the escapement to be damaged if a heavy pendulum causes the pallets to fall upon an idling escape wheel, which in a precision clock is likely to have delicate teeth. To overcome this, Harrison invented a form of maintaining power in the early eighteenth century (fig. 7). Its action is very simple in theory but not so easy to illustrate. The system works automatically. Two small but powerful springs are screwed to a large ratchet wheel, they act upon the spokes of this wheel and are therefore constantly under pressure. As the clock is being wound the pressure is released, the springs slowly uncoil by pushing the great wheel round and so they keep the clock going. This system may be used on weight-driven clocks and on fusée spring-driven clocks.

Compensated Pendulums

Metal expands and contracts with changes in atmospheric temperature, and of the two metals most commonly used in clock construction brass has a greater coefficient of expansion than steel. With an accurate regulator the very small changes in the length of a seconds pendulum would affect the rate of the clock if it were not fitted with a compensated pendulum.

George Graham invented the first temperature-compensated pendulum for use with his dead beat escapement. This is the mercury pendulum (fig. 8) which consists of a steel rod and the bob takes the form of a glass jar nearly filled with mercury. As the temperature rises the steel rod lengthens, but at the same time the mercury expands upwards in the jar so keeping the centre of oscillation constant. This method works extremely well when properly constructed, and was generally used for nineteenth-century English regulators.

The efforts made to produce an especially accurate timepiece in the early eighteenth century were partly to meet the requirements of astronomers who wished to time their observations to a split second. A reliable timekeeper was also needed for use on board ships to calculate their longitude when at sea. Both John and James Harrison

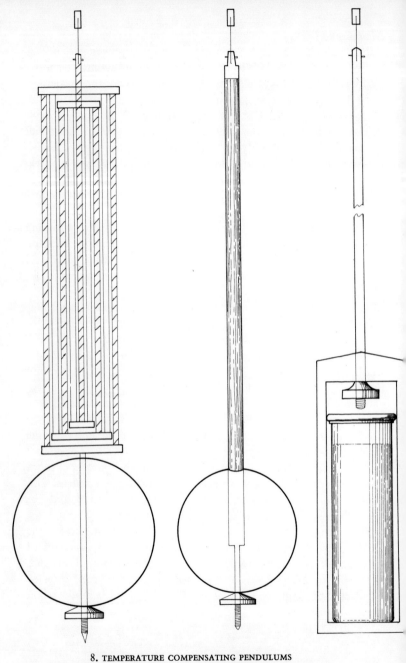

8. TEMPERATURE COMPENSATING PENDULUMS
HARRISON'S BI-METALLIC OR 'GRIDIRON' PENDULUM
WOOD ROD PENDULUM
GRAHAM'S MERCURIAL PENDULUM

spent much of their working lives perfecting such an instrument. To James Harrison is ascribed the invention of the popular gridiron-pendulum, used almost without exception on French regulators. As the drawing of this pendulum (fig. 8) shows, the steel rods are always longer than the brass ones. But, because the expansion of steel is less than that of brass, the greater expansion of the brass rods makes up for their shorter lengths and so keeps the length of the pendulum constant.

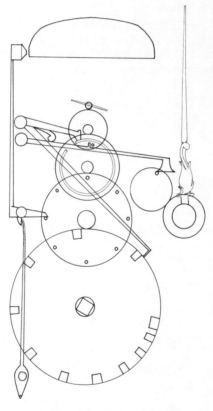

9. COUNTWHEEL STRIKING MECHANISM

Although this book is concerned only with domestic clocks, we will find that they sometimes incorporate escapements and pendulums devised for use on regulators made for astronomical or other specialised purposes. A third type of compensating pendulum is more commonly used on domestic clocks than the mercury and gridiron ones: this is the wooden rod pendulum, which is cheap, effective and has a lead or cast-iron bob. The wood must always be well-seasoned, with perfectly straight grain.

Striking Mechanisms
The countwheel or locking plate type of striking mechanism (fig. 9) was used on the very earliest clocks and continued in use well into the nineteenth century. To the striking train is geared a disk with notches cut in its perimeter. The notches are cut at an increasing distance from

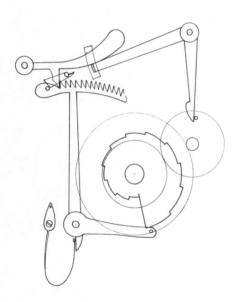

10. RACK STRIKING MECHANISM
INVENTED BY EDWARD
BARLOW IN 1676

one another for the hours one to twelve. Once the striking train is released by the going train, the clock continues to strike until the lever falls back into the next notch in the countwheel. With this system it is possible for the number of hours struck to become out of sequence with that indicated by the hand on the dial. This can usually only be remedied by releasing the striking mechanism manually and letting it sound each hour until it is back in phase with the hands. With a countwheel strike, it is thus impossible to have a pull-repeat mechanism to sound the last hour.

In 1676 the Reverend Edward Barlow invented a system known as the rack and snail (fig. 10), which makes it impossible for the hour struck to become out of sequence with the hands. The hour hand carries with it, behind the dial plate, a stepped snail-shaped disk, each step corresponding to an hour. At the hour the depth of the step determines how far the rack will fall and consequently how many teeth of the rack are to be gathered in again by the striking train. Each tooth gathered represents one stroke of the bell.

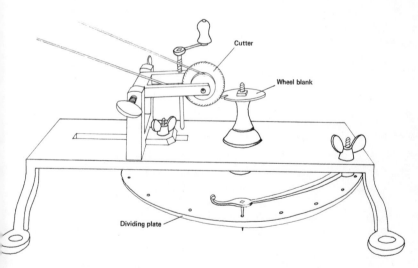

Cutter

Wheel blank

Dividing plate

11. WHEEL CUTTING MACHINE OF THE EIGHTEENTH CENTURY

2 *Germany, Austria, Switzerland*

Gothic Chamber Clocks

After the public or turret clock had become established, scaled-down versions began to be made for domestic use. The earliest domestic chamber clocks had only an hour-hand as they were not sufficiently accurate for a minute-hand to be worthwhile. Sometimes the dial was made with small knobs or 'touch pieces' at each hour so that the time could be felt by hand at night. Some chamber clocks stood on solid brackets fixed to the wall, but many were too heavy and stood on a pedestal on the floor. The earliest surviving chamber clocks date back to *c.* 1400.

Plate 1 – This sixteenth-century chamber clock still closely resembles a turret clock in construction. It stands about 60 cm (2 ft) high and is made entirely of iron. The foliot is clearly visible with its adjustable weights. Like all medieval chamber clocks, the four posts of the frame are made to resemble the buttresses of a church topped by pinnacle-like finials. The framework and the cruciform-shaped plates between which the wheels are pivoted are all fixed together by means of wedges. The hours are struck on the large bell. The alarm mechanism can be clearly seen mounted in one corner of the movement. The alarm hammer is mounted on the end of a verge staff and actuated by a crown wheel. Within the centre of the dial is a toothed wheel to which the hour-hand is fixed. To set the alarm, a peg is pushed into one of the twelve holes in this wheel. As the wheel rotates the peg lifts a lever which releases the alarm.

Perhaps the best-known clocks of the period were produced in Switzerland by the Liechti family. Until the seventeenth century most of their work was signed and dated, a practice which makes the study of antique clocks very much easier. The first clockmaking member of this family was born in 1480 and the business continued through twelve generations until 1857. Their early Gothic clocks are normally very decorative with elaborately painted dials. Every part of these old clocks was made by hand including the wheels, each tooth of which was scribed and cut or filed by hand. The wheels usually consist of two separate parts. The circular rim into which the teeth are cut is riveted or jointed onto the spokes which in turn are riveted or pinned to the arbor. It was not until the second half of the seventeenth century that wheel cutting machines, which divided and cut the teeth of the wheel in one operation, were widely used.

The Guilds of Southern Germany

In southern Germany the towns of Nuremberg and Augsburg were the unrivalled centres of clockmaking. In the early records of Nuremberg, fifteenth- and sixteenth-century clockmakers were referred to as locksmiths, because they were apprenticed to this trade and were members of the locksmiths' guild. In 1565, however, three craftsmen who made watches requested the city fathers to allow them to create a masterpiece which would confirm watchmaking as a separate craft. Their wishes were granted on condition the pieces were completed within one year. The first test piece was to be a clock or watch small enough to hang from a cord around a man's neck, it was to strike the hours and contain an alarm mechanism. Such watches were not small by our standards, being up to three inches in diameter. They were, in fact, miniature table clock movements.

The second piece was to be a tabernacle or belfry clock (plate 2). This was to show the twenty-four hours of the day and night, the quarter hours and the moon's phases. At the rear of the clock was to be an annual calendar dial, a planetary dial and another showing the changing lengths of the day and night. These requirements laid great stress on complexity, with no mention of accuracy. The

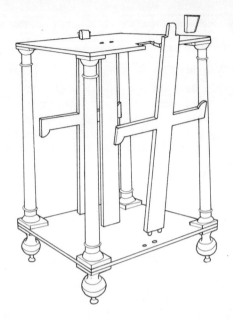

12. FOUR POSTER FRAME SHOWING METHOD OF REMOVING 'CRUCIFORM' PLATES

requirements were later altered and required the tabernacle clock to show the minutes, strike the hours and contain an astrolabe as well as an alarm mechanism.

This demand for elaborate dialwork and the strict guild laws led to the decline of the German industry and, by the eighteenth century, France and England had taken the lead.

The Renaissance

As the sixteenth century progressed more and more artists, designers and craftsmen absorbed the ideas of the Italian Renaissance. As a result, Gothic chamber clocks were made alongside weight- and spring-driven clocks of a distinctly classical style.

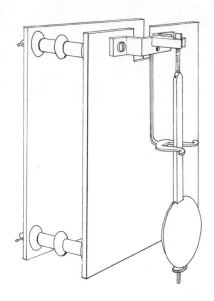

13. PLATED CONSTRUCTION OF
CLOCK MOVEMENT

Augsburg, a town in Bavaria, was perhaps the chief centre of clockmaking in Europe during the Renaissance. The quality of workmanship was consistently high, while the cases show great individuality and variety of design. Clocks were rarely signed although they often bear the town's stamps A.G. or a pineapple. At this period makers usually used their initials when signing a piece of work.

Spring-driven clocks can be easily classified by the construction of the movement. First there is the 4-post method of construction. Here the frame of the movement is a fixed unit and the vertical plates in which the wheels are pivoted and fitted into the frame by means of wedges. Secondly there is the plated method of construction. Here the plates in which the wheels are pivoted form part of the framework and are separated by decoratively turned pillars. One end of the pillar is riveted into one plate and the other plate is secured to the opposite end of the pillar by tapper pins. The advantage of the plated movement is that it can be very compact, since both sets of wheels can be laid out between the same two plates. At first they were placed horizontally with the dial on top of the clock.

A type of clock often associated with southern Germany, particularly Augsburg, is the so-called belfry or tabernacle clock. As the name implies, it takes the form of a tower. There are also examples from Austria, Italy and Holland which date from the mid-sixteenth century to the early eighteenth century.

14. A SIXTEENTH-CENTURY
TABLE CLOCK WITH A
DETACHABLE ALARM
MECHANISM. THE HAND
TRIPS A LEVER TO SET OFF
THE ALARM BELL

Plate 2 – An Augsburg table clock of the early seventeenth century, of the belfry or tabernacle type. The gilt brass case is modelled on classical architecture. The main dial shows mean solar time and lunar time. The phases of the moon can be seen in a circular aperture in the disk carrying the moon pointers. The centre of the dial is an astrolabe and shows the position of the sun, moon and a number of other stars in the heavens. The lower left-hand dial shows the Dominical Letter for the year and the number of the year in the solar cycle. On the left side of the clock is a small dial to indicate which quarter was last sounded, while on the right side is another dial to show which hour was last struck. The large dial on the rear of the clock originally gave the minutes and the hours on the 2 × 12 system, and also Italian hours. Small dials also on the rear of the clock show the day of the week and the position of the sun in the zodiac.

The movement was originally controlled by a balance wheel. After the invention of the pendulum in 1657 many clocks, including this one, were converted to pendulum control. The pendulum clock was a prized object and so the pendulum was often made to swing in front of the dial where all could see it.

Many clocks made before the eighteenth century show the time on two or three dials. In Europe there were three methods of counting the hours. By the late sixteenth century the double twelve-hour count had become almost universal, except in Rome where a six-hour dial was used and in Germany where the twenty-four-hour dial was used.

Plate 3a – A German drum-shaped table clock made *c.* 1580. The dial has an outer ring of roman numerals from 1–12 and an inner ring of arabic numerals 13–24. It is also fitted with touch knobs for feeling the time in the dark. Such clocks were sometimes supplied or fitted with a detachable alarm mechanism (fig. 14). The movement of a drum clock may be controlled by a balance wheel or by what is called a 'dumb-bell' balance, which is a minute foliot looking like a dumb-bell.

The Baroque

During the seventeenth century the classical lines of the Renaissance gave way to the elaborate and vigorous designs of the Baroque which developed most vigorously, and even excessively, in Germany. The inventiveness of the German designers is particularly illustrated in the clock cases. Some have a globe supported on a pillar or by a group of youths, with the hour numerals on the globe rotating past a fixed pointer. Similar clocks represent Christ on the cross, or the Virgin and Child surmounted by a crown on which are the hour numerals.

Plate 4 – A novelty clock in the form of a globe mounted on the trunk of a palm tree. This early seventeenth-century clock is basically a drum-shaped table clock on an elaborately moulded base. The hour-hand arbor is mounted off-centre and continues up the trunk of the tree, on the end of which is the globe bearing the hour numerals. As the hour strikes, the man's head moves and the dog at his feet moves as if running.

Plate 5 – An early seventeenth-century clock case of novel design from southern Germany. Many such animal clocks have the animal standing or seated upon an ebony case with little windows on each side. At each hour the griffon's wings flap and its beak opens and closes. The brass tube running into its chest drives the mechanism animating the bird. By its feet are dials to show which hour and quarter-hour were last struck.

Other clocks even used their own weight to turn the wheels. The rack clock is an example of this. A drum-shaped clock is mounted over a toothed vertical pillar. To wind it, the clock is lifted to the top of the rack and its descent is regulated by the escapement.

The most excessive design of the Baroque was the 'Prunk Uhr' or cabinet clock. This was occasionally so elaborate that it became a sizeable piece of furniture incorporating numerous little cupboards and secret compartments; usually, however, it stood upon a stand or table. Most were made of wood or metal, but some are masterpieces of the silversmith's art: set with precious and semi-precious stones, embossed, engraved or enamelled. They are often decorated with groups of twisted columns supporting a massive superstructure of balustrades, pediments and figures which symbolise the arts or Roman gods. The movements are seldom as complicated as those

26

of tabernacle clocks. Sometimes the dial or dials are so insignificant that it takes a few moments to recognise that what one is looking at is indeed a clock.

The Thirty Years' War, which began in 1618 between Catholics and Protestants, so disrupted life in Germany that between 1618 and 1645 the number of clockmakers in Augsburg dwindled from forty-three to seven. During this same period the French centres of Blois, Lyon and Paris, and the Swiss and English centres of Geneva and London, were growing rapidly.

Small table clocks, very often hexagonal in shape, were still made in the early eighteenth century, two hundred years after their first appearance. These later clocks are in less decorative cases, with badly proportioned mouldings. They usually have little windows in their sides and have a minute as well as an hour-hand.

Plate 3b – An hexagonal table clock about 12 cm (5 in) in width. Notice the champlevé chapter ring. This is where the depth of the chapter ring is reduced between the numerals, the lower portions usually being matted. The champlevé dial must not be confused with the skeleton chapter ring where areas of the ring between the numerals are cut out completely. One of the spring barrels can be seen through the bevelled glass window and is covered with engraving, while the hour bell can just be seen, mounted below the movement. Similar clocks were also made in Austria and many have fictitious London makers' names engraved upon the dial.

The Eighteenth Century

The eighteenth century was a time of a great expansion in the clock-making industry in Austria, especially in Vienna, and in Switzerland, which concentrated mainly on watch production. Augsburg was not the great centre it had once been, but its influence was still widely felt. A form of clock which had been made in Augsburg as far back as the early seventeenth century was the Teller Uhr or plate clock, so called because of the shape and nature of its dial. These were made in southern Germany and Austria until the late eighteenth century.

The Teller Uhr, which hangs from a hook on the wall, had a spring-driven movement controlled by a watch escapement or later by a

27

cow's tail pendulum, a short pendulum which swings in front of the dial. The dial can vary from about 15 cm (6 in) to 45 cm (18 in) in diameter. Many are surrounded by an embossed and sometimes silvered brass plate, while the seventeenth-century examples may have no surround at all. The Zappler is a very similar clock, but it is made to stand on a table or cabinet top and was made well into the nineteenth century. The later Viennese makers often made small examples, some of them no more than a few centimetres high. Like carriage clocks, both the Zappler and the Teller Uhr have become specialised areas of collecting.

English clocks were very highly regarded throughout Europe in the early eighteenth century and the work of leading makers was not only copied but their proportions and design had a noticeable influence on the work of many Austrian and German makers.

Plate 6 – This clock shows how English bracket clock design was interpreted by Austrian makers of the late eighteenth century. The fruitwood case has a brass carrying handle, four finials and brass feet. All other gilt ornamentation on the case is of carved wood. The brass dial is signed 'Ge. Preisacher, Clostemenburg'. The arch contains a large calendar dial with the signs of the zodiac. The two subsidiary dials are for strike/silent and chime/silent. The backplate is engraved with a central cartouche of scrolls and foliage. The case is quite shallow compared to those of contemporary English bracket clocks.

Plate 7 – A good example of the kind of bracket clock produced in Austria and southern Germany during the latter half of the eighteenth century. The maker, Adalbertus Hockenadl, was one of a family of Viennese clockmakers who also sold, and possibly even made, clocks in Venice. This example is signed 'Venetia'. As is usual with Austrian bracket clocks it has only a 40-hour movement. The going train has a chain fusée, while the chiming part has a gut fusée. The striking train, however, has a going barrel; such a mixture is common in Austrian work. The going barrel is fitted with stop-work so that it cannot be overwound. The movement has heavy rectangular plates and is closer to English work of the period than to French. As well as chiming the quarter-hours on eight bells it has an alarm mechanism. The dials in the arch are for chime/silent and pendulum regulation.

The pendulum hangs upon a silk suspension. The chapter ring is secured by four tiny screws, a feature never found on English and seldom on French work. Austrian clocks often have the dial centre engraved to match the engraving in the arch. The painted wooden case with its sprays of flowers and blue interior is particularly beautiful. Ebonised, walnut veneered and marquetry cases were also popular.

Another major influence was the rococo, which is best illustrated by the Swiss Neuchâtel bracket clocks, named after the horological centre of that country. These eighteenth-century clocks were copies of the waisted French bracket clock in plate 29. Later a more individual style, with restrained gilt mounts, evolved. The case of wood was often lacquered and decorated with flowers or *chinoiserie*.

P. Jaquet-Droz of Neuchâtel made superb bracket clocks in the French style and in some of them he is known to have included complicated chiming and musical movements. Both Pierre and his son Henri became celebrated clock, watch and automaton makers. Many complicated watches were exported to China in the late eighteenth century, as well as wonderful automata such as that of a human figure who can write with pen and ink upon paper. Henri also worked in collaboration with Henri Maillardet from 1775, who was a member of another distinguished clock- and automata-making family, much of whose work also went to China. Henri Maillardet devised a single whistle with a moving piston to alter the note for mechanical singing birds, and with it was able to reproduce bird song almost perfectly.

In the last quarter of the century high quality machine-made watches began to be made in Switzerland. F. Japy was the first to manufacture watch *ébauches* by machines. In 1818 Japy opened a factory for the production of clock *ébauches* in Baderel.

The Swiss combined inventiveness, mechanical ingenuity and superb craftsmanship. Some of the leading makers in France and England such as Berthoud, Breguet, Recordon and Emery were, in fact, Swiss. By 1800 the Swiss industry had overtaken England and France in the production of watches of quality, which were also cheaper and more compact. During the nineteenth century Switzerland secured a virtual monopoly of the Chinese market. Many watches had elaborate repeating mechanisms which made figures on the dial strike little bells. Others contained minute musical box movements which played a tune at the hour or at will.

Plate 8 – A Swiss bracket clock or Neuchâteloise of the early nineteenth century. This style of clock evolved in the Neuchâtel district of Switzerland. The case sits upon a matching wall bracket. The cast brass bezel around the dial and that surrounding the pendulum aperture are in one piece. The long plain pointer on the enamelled dial is the alarm setting hand. The rear of the case can be removed to gain access to the movement. The movement of this clock has *grande sonnerie* striking, that is it sounds each quarter on two gongs and the last hour on a bell. All the lifting levers and racks for the chiming are mounted on the back plate.

There were no craftsmen of the influence of Sheraton or Adam in Germany and so clock case design was influenced by both English and French styles in the eighteenth century and many local styles also developed. Both longcase and bracket clocks were popular in Germany. Like the French and Dutch the *bombé* base was much used on longcase clocks. Veneers were often inlaid in panels of parquetrie, and the trunks were often shaped, swelling in rococo curves at the level of the pendulum bob. By the 1750s most German states had adopted the French rococo style. The fashionable court of the Elector of Bavaria at Munich, for instance, employed craftsmen trained in Paris. The famous Roentgen workshops at Neuwied produced some of the most beautiful furniture.

Abraham Roentgen, 1711–93, worked in Holland and England in his early years, and his son, David, later had considerable influence on German furniture. His designs were light and graceful and not over-elaborate. Many of his longcase clock cases display very fine pictorial marquetry on the trunk and base. The designs for this inlay (a specialty of his) were often taken from the paintings of Januarious Zick.

Clockcases by Roentgen usually contain movements by Kinzing. In one clock made by this partnership in 1805 Kinzing used Benjamin Franklin's unique dial layout. This uses one hand which makes one

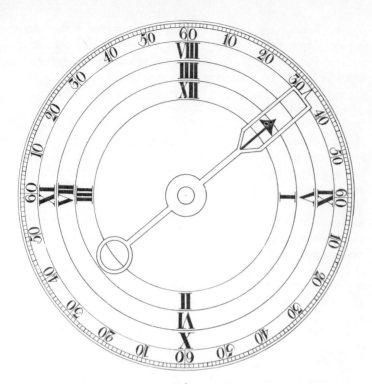

15. THE DIAL OF BENJAMIN FRANKLIN'S ONE-HANDED CLOCK AS MADE BY
SEVERAL MAKERS IN GERMANY AND ENGLAND

revolution of the dial every four hours, and shows the minutes. It also has a 'window' along its length in which is another pointer indicating the hours. This second pointer adjusts itself to the appropriate ring after each 4-hour period.

The idea of the picture clock is a very old one, since it is known that as early as 1700 a certain Friedrick Christian Hirt made clocks fitted into church towers within landscape paintings. In the early nineteenth century the Swiss cashed in on this idea which the French were making popular. Characteristically the Swiss were seldom content to make do with an ordinary striking movement and often fitted a comb musical box which played a tune every hour.

Nineteenth-century Vienna

Viennese clocks echoed both the French rococo and the neoclassical styles. Gilt cartel clocks were a popular type, but instead of being of cast bronze they were made of carved and gilt wood, like those in England. Carved and gilt wood mantel clocks were also made towards the end of the eighteenth century in the neoclassical designs fashionable in Paris. The gilt is often of several shades and burnished in parts. The dials are usually enamelled and the 30-hour movements often chime and repeat the quarter-hours at will. It is not unusual to find examples with sweep-centre calendar hands.

The nineteenth century saw a considerable growth in the Viennese industry, partly due to the increased export trade to eastern Europe and Italy. Large numbers of mantel clocks made at this time were variations of the four-pillar or portico style of case seen in plate 36. Mahogany and ebonised cases were particularly popular, with columns of alabaster, glass or gilt wood framing mirror glasses or even delicate paintings by artists such as Wiegand, who painted architectural subjects. The dials may be of engine-turned brass, or enamelled. Sometimes, on especially fine pieces, the centre of the dial may feature an automaton scene set off as the clock strikes. Another particularly charming feature is the musical box fitted in the base of some clocks which is set off by the clock at the hour. The disadvantage of so many Viennese clocks is that they are only of 30-hour duration. Only special 'one off' pieces were of 8-day duration.

Plate 9 – An Empire or Biedermeier period mantel clock of about 1825 standing 45·7 cm (18 in) high. The case, which is designed as an obelisk on a plinth, is of mahogany with ebony mouldings and brass mounts. The enamelled dial has Breguet style hands and a centre calendar pointer. It is signed 'Niederlags Compagnie in Wien' and has a quarter-striking movement. The pendulum regulation square can be seen over the figure twelve.

The clock for which Vienna is renowned is, of course, the Vienna regulator, a name used indiscriminately today to describe any wall regulator with glass front and sides even if it is a mass-produced article from the U.S.A. or Germany. The movements are of fine quality and were secured to the back of the case by cast brass brackets. The pendulum was also suspended from a bracket on the back board and not from the back plate of the movement. Many of these clocks are not true regulators since they also strike the hour or even chime the quarters. Even so they are all fitted with temperature-compensating pendulums, a dead beat escapement and maintaining power.

Plate 10 – This is a striking Vienna regulator movement of the second half of the nineteenth century and is typical of Austrian work. It is instructive to compare this with movements of a similar period made in France (plate 37), England (plate 57), and America (plate 73). English movements of the period are extremely weighty while American movements are very flimsy. Austrian work is closest to that of France.

Plate 11a – A longcase regulator in a burr walnut case with inlaid lines of contrasting white wood. The inside of the case is also finely veneered. The sides of the case have windows as well as the hood and trunk. The severe architectural style of the case is typical of the first quarter of the nineteenth century. The clock has a massive pendulum bob and wooden rod which, like pendulums on all Vienna regulators, swings through an exceedingly small arc. The glass dial is not uncommon on Vienna regulators. The counter-balanced minute- and hour-hands are in the form of arrows. In a sense this clock is not a true regulator since it strikes the hours and also chimes the quarters. The clock stands slightly over 1·8 m (6 ft) high. In the background is a reproduction of a late 18th-century Neuchâtel bracket clock in a red lacquer case with matching wall bracket and brass mounts.

Plate 11b – A wall regulator dating from the latter half of the nineteenth century. Early nineteenth-century wall regulators were designed like the longcase clock in plate 11a with a hood trunk and glazed base in which the pendulum bob swung. The ebonised case of this clock is conceived as a single unit enlivened by finials and a central cresting. The dial is of two pieces with a recessed centre.

3

Black Forest

The Black Forest area of Germany includes the provinces of Baden and Württemberg bordered to the south and west by the Rhine. The northern border of Switzerland is included within the area which is referred to as the Black Forest school of clockmaking.

The hard winters which the area experiences encouraged local people to find new indoor occupations, and by the second half of the seventeenth century a cottage clockmaking industry was established. The area had always been known for its glass manufacture, and some clocks may even be found with glass bells. In an area such as the Black Forest there was a great tradition of woodworking and carving and it was to this material that the clockmakers naturally turned. The local timber is mainly coniferous, and it is probable that much of the hardwood used for the intricate work of making the plates and wheels was imported. The dials and side doors were the only parts made of the local soft woods. The plates, arbors and (on early examples) the wheels were made of beech.

The tools which the craftsmen used were as unusual as the construction of the wooden movements. The region has some fine museums (such as those at Furtwangen and Triberg) where one can see both the clocks and also reconstructions of typical nineteenth-century clockmakers' workshops, complete with lathes and wheelcutting machines constructed mostly of wood to individual designs. The massiveness of these treadle-operated machines with their heavy stone flywheels produced a very sure and steady action.

As in any clockmaking community, no one man made a complete clock. Much of the work would be done in farmers' cottages, collected and assembled in larger workshops. Each man would specialise in the production of a particular part, so there would be dial makers, dial painters, frame makers, chain makers and so on.

Like the clocks produced in the Morbier district of France, designs varied little over many generations. The foliot, for example, was probably used until as late as the 1740s. Few early clocks have survived and it is rare to come across an eighteenth-century example. It is very difficult to date these clocks with any accuracy, since styles changed so slowly. Towards the close of the eighteenth century brass began to be produced locally, and this was used for making the wheels.

Plate 12a – This movement is of the mid-nineteenth century. The brass wheels are mounted on wooden arbors often painted to imitate steel. The pivots are of wire set in brass bushes sunk into the wooden plates. The pinions are of the lantern form, with wire leaves. The striking is the countwheel type.

Plate 12b – It is interesting to see how the clocks were fitted with different dials to suit the taste of the country to which they were to be exported. The shield dial on this clock was the traditional design which was popular in the Low Countries and with the French, who liked them gaily painted with flowers in the spandrels. This one is only 20·3 cm (8 in) high. The movement is an alarm timepiece although the central alarm disk is not original.

Hexagonal dials were favoured in Scandinavia, while those exported to England were mostly in the style of the English fusée dial clock. Some of the more elaborate cases were made in England to house these Black Forest movements.

The Black Forest clocks have often been mistakenly called Dutch clocks, a corruption of the word Deutsch. These clocks were sold by travelling salesmen. Each salesman would hire a room and have a number of clocks delivered there. He would then set out each day carrying his wares on a *tragstuhl*, a form of carrying frame. These travelling salesmen became the subject of a clock, made of painted cast iron, where one of their number is seen carrying two clocks, one of which contains a miniature verge spring-driven movement. Good reproductions of these clocks are now being made.

Another notable miniature was the weight-driven Jockel clock. The pendulum swings outside the case, which is kept a centimetre or two away from the wall by wooden spikes. The dials are normally of fired enamel surmounted or surrounded by a repoussé brass shield.

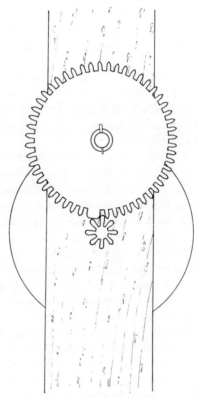

16. STOP WORK ON BLACK
FOREST SPRING–DRIVEN
CLOCKS

Late nineteenth century Jockel clocks were also made with dainty porcelain cases.

Quarter-chiming clocks were made with elaborately shaped arch dials and an aperture in which figures can be seen striking the bells.

Another elaborate clock was the cuckoo clock, invented in about 1730 by Anton Ketterer of Schonwald, but it did not gain universal popularity until the nineteenth century. The bird sound is produced by small bellows blowing air through the wooden pipes, like an organ. Ketterer never knew that the cuckoo clock was eventually to become the most famous product of the Black Forest. The cuckoo clocks of about 1800–20 were simply wooden shield dials with a little door in the arch where the bird appears.

Plate 12c – By the mid-nineteenth century more elaborate examples appeared with the movement completely enclosed within a soundly made case. The clock illustrated has a chalet style case with brass inlaid lines. The painted dial surround is of tin, the dial itself is enamelled on copper.

To have the striking train positioned behind the going train of weight-driven clocks resulted in a very deep frame, which subsequently tended to twist the movement out of shape (see plate 12a). To overcome this some clocks were made with the trains mounted side-by-side.

Competition from America
The export trade flourished until Jerome and other American factories began to export cheap clocks in sophisticated-looking cases to Europe. From about 1845 competition became increasingly tough, and eventually the Black Forest was forced to turn to mass production techniques.

The success of American and French spring-driven clocks may have tempted Black Forest makers to introduce spring-driven wall clocks.

Plate 12d – This is a wooden plated 8-day spring-driven wall clock. It is fitted with stop work to avoid overwinding (see diagram). Some of these clocks, especially mantle clocks, were even fitted with fusées. The case is veneered in walnut with brass inlaid lines and is a close copy of English wall clocks. One way to distinguish a Black Forest-made case from an English one is that the Black Forest case will have a removable back to allow access to the movement. The zinc dial painted cream, is signed 'Beha Lickert & Co. of Norwich' who was the retailer of the clock.

Mass Production

To match American competition, factory production was started in the 1850s in Schwenningen by Johannes Burk, followed soon after by Erhard Junghans at Schramberg. Junghan's brother had actually worked in an American clock factory and was able to bring valuable information to the family business. Their clocks were exact replicas of American products except that instead of rolled brass for the plates and stamped out wheels, the Germans used castings which were heavier and show the marks of hand finishing.

The idea of making American clocks in Germany was taken to extraordinary lengths. Printed labels showing the factories or coats of arms were pasted inside the cases, and printed and coloured designs were applied to the glass panels below the dials. Even the numerous companies which grew up took on American-sounding names, such as the Teutonia Clock Manufactory, The Hamburg American Clock Co., and the Union Clock Co. Often it is very difficult to differentiate between the products of the two countries.

Plate 13a – Three German clocks of typical American shelf clock form. The left-hand one is by the Union Clock Co. of Furtwangen and is the closest to its American prototypes. The case is painted with false rosewood graining and is decorated with gilt mouldings. The zinc dial is not painted but is faced with printed paper; note the shaped centre and the alarm disk. The right-hand clock is displayed with the dial removed to show the mass-produced movement and the label of the Union Clock Co. This clock was probably made in the early 1900s. The movement in the centre clock is of finer quality. It has solid cast brass plates stamped 'W. & H. Sch.' for Winterhalder and Hoffmeier of Schramberg, and also has stop work. It was retailed in England by Camerer Kuss and Co. who had premises in New Oxford St., Bloomsbury, and Shepherd's Bush, London. Their label

38

advertises 'a large assortment of curiosity and cuckoo clocks always on sale'. This clock in its sombre ebonised case probably dates from the 1880s.

Many popular styles of American clocks were copied by German factories. They also produced cheap copies of the very popular Vienna regulator, many fitted with spring-driven movements and sham gridiron pendulums. The popularity of these wall clocks helped to kill the Dutch clockmaking industry which, like the English, was too slow and reluctant to change its production methods. Junghan's also made longcase clocks after 1900. The models with chiming movements playing on gongs sold well in England. They had glass doors through which could be seen the brass pendulum bob and weights. The movements of most German clocks made in the years leading up to World War I were of good quality despite being mass-produced; indeed some of them approached the quality of French clocks, with heavy plates and well-cut wheels.

Plate 13b – A cuckoo clock of the second half of the nineteenth century. It has a brass movement and heavily carved case in the form of oak, ivy or vine leaves inhabited by birds and animals. The white-painted hands may not be original. Many carved cuckoo clocks were originally fitted with matching carved wood pendulum bobs.

Plate 13c – This is a typical cuckoo clock movement of cast brass from the second half of the nineteenth century. It is quite easy to see the file marks where the rough castings were finished. The pipes which produce the bird sound are to the left and right of the movement, the little bellows above each are actuated by wires from the striking train.

Plate 14 – Even in the 1900s, when mass production was the rule rather than the exception, wooden-plated movements were still being made. The most usual form was known as the postman's alarm, here seen with the dial painted on the reverse of a sheet of glass enabling it to be kept clean without damaging the numerals. This particular example was first purchased by a gentleman who worked for the Great Western Railway in Exeter, England, in 1914.

A very successful clock of novel design was the 400-day clock with a torsion pendulum invented by Anton Harder. The pendulum consists of a very fine brass strip from which hangs the slowly-turning balance. These clocks are housed under a glass dome and have sold in huge numbers and in dozens of slightly different designs from the 1880s to the present day. The same torsion principle was employed again in the Atmos clock (plate 42).

4 *Holland*

Like most European countries, Holland had an established clock-making trade by the Middle Ages. Examples do exist of Gothic weight-driven chamber clocks with the familiar features of 4-poster movements with buttress-shaped posts and tall, tapering pinnacle-like finials.

By the mid-seventeenth century Dutch chamber clocks were placed on purpose-built wooden brackets not unlike the Stoel clocks of a later period. The posts of the movement were of a truly classical architectural design – Tuscan columns standing upon square pedestals. Strangely, these beautiful columns were enclosed within the un-decorated side doors and do not form a part of the external design. In this respect there is a link with the so-called lantern clocks of Japan.

The Invention of the Pendulum

The Hague was to earn a reputation for itself during the latter part of the seventeenth century since it was near where Christian Huygens, the scientist, worked. By the age of twenty-six, in 1655, he had already discovered a new satellite of Saturn with a telescope which he had constructed himself, and it was to assist his astronomical observations that he turned his mind to making an improved timepiece. He was also concerned with producing a clock which would function well enough aboard ship to be used for finding longitude and so improve navigation.

Although Huygens was not the first to use a pendulum to control clockwork he was certainly responsible for its successful application in Holland, France and England. He constructed his first model in 1656 and within the following months Solomon Coster, a clockmaker who worked for Huygens, took out a patent on the new invention, which gave him sole rights to make and sell pendulum clocks in the Netherlands for twenty-one years. Huygens probably took a share of the profits. The granting of this patent may explain why the Dutch industry did not expand as fast as would be expected at this time. Huygens also tried to secure a patent for his invention in France but his requests were repeatedly refused. The French, especially Parisians, ordered many pendulum clocks from makers in the Hague, but by 1662 Huygens himself admitted that the French were making superior clocks to those of the Dutch, especially regarding finish. By this date it is possible that French taste was demanding a more ornate article than the Dutch were making.

Plates 15 and 16 – This clock is very similar to the first pendulum clocks made in the Hague, from where its name, Haagse clock, originates. It is signed 'Van Ceulen' and dates from about 1675. The going and striking trains are both driven from one spring. The pendulum is suspended between curved 'cycloidal cheeks'. When these cheeks are of the correct curvature the pendulum describes a cycloidal arc and not the arc of a circle. In this cycloidal arc the time of each swing of the pendulum is equal, regardless of the size of the arc of the swing. Very few clockmakers fully understood this principle and many makers fitted curved cheeks although they were of the wrong shape. Notice the beautifully decorated wings to the back cock and the pierced frets to the striking lifting and locking piece arbors. The dial is hinged to the case to allow easy access to the movement. The chapter ring, supported by a figure of Father Time, is cut out or skeletonised and each minute is engraved around its edge. Notice that the bell is not fitted to the movement but is mounted on top of the case, behind the open arched pediment. The rings on the back of the case are to secure the clock to the wall, but it could equally well be used as a table clock.

Plate 17 – A magnificent silver-cased clock, with a movement by Adriaen Van den Bergh of the Hague, and a case signed J. H. C. Breghtel. The extremely elaborate case displays more German than

Dutch characteristics and must surely have been inspired by the decorative pieces of Augsburg and Nuremberg. The silver case which stands about 75 cm (2 ft 6 in) high is covered with fretted and engraved silver of an intricate floral design. The clock has dials on two sides and was evidently intended to stand in the centre of the room, or at least somewhere where all sides could be seen.

Plate 18 – At first sight this clock could easily be mistaken for an English production. It is by Roger Dunster, who was evidently so well-known that he thought it unnecessary to mention on the dial that he worked in Amsterdam. This clock is of about 1745 and is very like the fine clocks made by Benjamin Gray and Vulliamy in London at this time. Within the arch is a pendulum regulation dial, a large calendar dial and a strike/silent lever. The central alarm disk is very typically Dutch. The clock is controlled by a short pendulum and verge escapement; the false pendulum aperture above the centre of the dial shows that the clock is going and can be used to set the pendulum in motion after rewinding.

English designs at this period had a great influence on Dutch makers, especially in the field of bracket clocks where there was no traditional Dutch design.

The idea of fraudulently engraving famous makers' names onto clock dials is by no means a modern one. In 1704 the master of the London clockmakers' company complained that 'certain persons at Amsterdam were in the habit of putting the names of Tompion, Windmills, Quare, Cabrier, Lamb and other well-known London makers on their works and selling them as English'.

Weight-driven Wall Clocks

The Zaanse clock, believed to have originated in the Zaan region, is probably the earliest of the numerous styles of wall clock. The weight-driven wall clock was without question the most popular clock in Holland, the longcase and bracket clocks being made mostly in the cities. The movements of Zaanse clocks are usually quite simple, while the strap-type frame can be traced back to medieval clocks. To dismantle the framework a wedge is removed from the hinged top plate. Zaanse clocks may date back to the 1650s and have verge

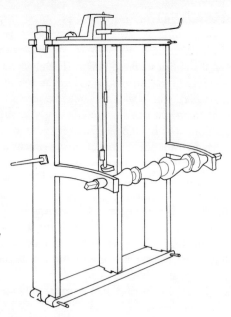

17. STRAP FORM OF CONSTRUCTION OF THE ZAANSE CLOCK SHOWING HOW MOVEMENT IS HINGED AND WEDGED TOGETHER. ALSO SHOWN IS THE VERGE STAFF AND CRUTCH

escapements. The verge staff is placed vertically, as it would be if the clock had a balance wheel, and is connected to the pendulum by a long wire. The pendulum is contained within the box-like wall bracket which is usually elaborately shaped. This wall bracket supports the wooden cased clock itself. The case sits upon turned feet and often has twisted baroque columns at the corners. Examples with arched dials and moon work appear to have been made in the seventeenth century, pre-dating the popularity of the arch dial in England by a good twenty years. The cases are invariably surmounted by very ornate cast brass crestings, the front one often incorporating an arched open pediment on which stand figures of Faith, Hope and Charity.

Inside the crestings are the two bells for the hours and half hours on which stand the figure of Atlas or Minerva. Zaanse clocks usually have pear-shaped brass-cased weights suspended on a rope.

Plate 19 – Two Zaanse clocks. The one on the left is signed 'Groot 1725'. The simple turned corner columns to the case support a horizontal entablature surmounted by the normal metal cresting. The dial is velvet covered, onto which are applied a wide chapter-ring and cherub's head spandrels. A similar clock is seen to the right but this has a painted dial plate.

A more common type of wall clock is the Stoel clock or little chair clock, so-called because the 4-poster movement sits upon a wooden stool supported by the wall bracket. This type of clock was made in large numbers in Freisland – the northern part of Holland. The polished wood cases of the Zaanse clocks are quite sombre compared with the Stoel clocks which display a mass of gaily coloured paint-work.

The movements of early eighteenth-century Stoel clocks are very similar to the movements of some mid-seventeenth-century wall clocks. During the eighteenth century the classical style of the corner posts gave way to more imaginative turning, similar to that of the Staart clock movement in plate 22.

Before 1750 the raised chapter ring of silvered brass was usually mounted on a painted dial plate which might depict landscape scenes, figures or flowers. Above and below the dial plate were pierced metal castings of leafy scrolls often incorporating heraldic motifs. The metal used, often lead, was always painted gold. Occasionally examples can be found with this kind of decoration sprouting from all four sides of the dial. The wall bracket itself was shaped on either side in the form of painted mermaids or vase handles. To the top of this wall board a canopy is fixed which may protect the movement from dust although its main function was decorative. While the weights of the Zaanse clock are normally hung on plaited ropes, those of the Stoel clock and Staart clock are hung on chains of a particular kind. Each link is a figure of eight with the two circles of the figure twisted at right angles to one another. In other words, one link of this chain corresponds to two links of a normal chain.

Plate 20 – A Stoel clock with a verge escapement positioned, as in a Zaanse clock, with a vertical verge staff. The 4-post movement has thin turned brass posts connecting the iron top and bottom plates. This clock does not strike the hours but has an alarm mechanism mounted on the rear of the back plate. The cast brass hour-hand has a large central boss on which are marked the hours for the small iron alarm pointer. The short pendulum is mounted from a peg on the back board.

The basic types of wall clock are fairly distinct, but there are transitional types which may have features of both Zaanse and Stoel or may appear to be a cross between Stoel and Staart clocks.

The Staart clock or tail clock is so named because of the great length of the wall board which is, like the Zaanse clock, of box-like construction to contain the pendulum. The Staart clock is a more refined and imposing clock than the Stoel clock which it eventually superseded. Its hood is like that of a longcase clock and the movement, which is similar to the Stoel clock movement, is bolted to a base board. Variations of the Staart clock were made, one with a short trunk is known as a *Kortkast*. Very small examples were made for use on the barges using Holland's inland waterways and these are known as little ships' clocks or *Schippertjes*. They have short pendulums within the hood and have verge escapements which performed better than the more usual anchor which would have been upset by the movement of the vessel. Staart clocks were made from the late eighteenth century to about 1880. The town of Joure seems to have been the main centre of their production, which was at its height in the mid-nineteenth century.

Plates 21 and 22 – A Staart clock in an oak case stained to simulate mahogany. The 30-hour movement has one brass-bound weight. The iron dial is elaborately painted, while under the chapter ring is a coastal scene with a rocking ship, a windmill with rotating sails and a fisherman whose rod is constantly rising and falling. The position of the automata scene is unusual, as it generally is in the arch. The movement (plate 22) shows that the countwheel is cut for Dutch double-striking. The hour is sounded on the larger bell, then at the half-hour it is sounded again on the smaller bell (a replacement). The automated ship and fisherman are actuated from the crutch to the pendulum, while the windmill is connected to a wooden pulley on the escape wheel arbor (the pulley on the windmill is a replacement and the pulley cord is missing).

It is almost impossible to date Staart clocks precisely, since they were made to the same design for nearly a century. This one is probably late eighteenth century or early nineteenth century.

Lastly under the heading of wall clocks must be mentioned the Amsterdamse hanging clocks. These clocks predate the Staart clock but are similar in concept; the most noticeable difference is in the movement. The movements of Amsterdamse hanging clocks are like those of good quality 30-hour longcase clocks. They are plated and have brass dials often with a seconds dial, alarm and moon phases in the arch. The hood is identical in design to good quality Amsterdam longcase clocks, usually veneered in walnut with an elaborate scroll top surmounted by a dome and figures of Atlas and trumpeting angels. The wall board contains the pendulum which is seen through a lenticle in the short door.

The Longcase Clock

While the wall clock was certainly the favourite clock of Holland, longcase clocks were made throughout the eighteenth century, first appearing in about 1680 and closely resembling English clocks of the period. The popular velvet-covered dial plate was used on many early examples. The hands of early Dutch longcase clocks are often very much finer than English examples. When the velvet overlay was used, the hands were of beautifully pierced, engraved and gilt brass, while the hands for dials with matt brass centres were of blued steel. The cases of late seventeenth-century longcase clocks were of walnut or covered in parquetry or marquetry designs.

Plate 23a – This clock marks the peak of the longcase clock and was made by Roger Dunster of Amsterdam, a leading eighteenth-century maker. The exotic-looking veneer is mulberry wood, which is inlaid with ebony stringing and has ebonised mouldings. The base has *bombé* sides. The cast brass mount to the lenticle on the trunk door figures the rape of Europa. The movement is a musical one, with a selection of twelve tunes and is similar to that seen in plate 24. Apart from the signature, the arch contains a painting of musicians in classical costume. This imposing piece is nearly 2·7 m (9 ft) high.

Plate 23b – Another fine longcase clock made in Amsterdam this time by Jan Van Brussel. The 8-day movement also shows the moon's phases in the arch. There is an alarm disk in the dial centre, and within the seconds dial is a square aperture showing the day of the month and below the dial centre is the day of the week. The finely veneered walnut case has a *bombé* base, common to much Dutch furniture of the mid-eighteenth century. The whole clock stands 2 m (7 ft) high.

Plate 24 – A musical longcase clock movement made by Franciscus Bavius of Leeuwarden, in northern Holland, in about 1760. The dial of this clock has subsidiary dials for strike/not strike and chime/not chime, and also has segment-shaped calendar apertures for the month and day of the week. The clock had two interchangeable musical barrels with twelve tunes on each. The musical longcase clock was very much more popular in Holland than in England, where even a clock which chimes the quarter-hours is a rarity. By mounting the musical barrel horizontally across the back plate, it was possible to accommodate this movement within a case of fine proportions a little larger than a normal case. There are two hammers to each bell which allows one note to be repeated in very quick succession to produce lively and interesting tunes. The hours are struck on the large bell nestling between the dial and the musical bells, and the half-hours are struck on the smaller bell mounted on the back plate.

The wall clock outlived the longcase in popularity since the Staart clock was still made in very large numbers in the 1850s. This was just the time when cheap and mass-produced American and Black Forest clocks were beginning to arrive in England and Holland in large numbers. These low-priced clocks were, however, surprisingly reliable and would keep reasonable time and were consequently most popular with working people. The middle classes also bought the more elegant and decorative mass-produced imports.

According to E. J. Tyler in *European Clocks*, Dutch retailers encouraged demand for German-made clocks by giving a rebate on old Dutch clocks brought in for part exchange. The heavy brass movements were then sold as scrap metal, the cases (even today) sold for firewood and movements thrown away by the ill-informed. In my own experience no fine old movement or shattered case is beyond restoration and is always well worth the effort and expense.

5 *France*

The Renaissance

It is the spring-driven clocks which have survived best of the clocks of the sixteenth century. Because they are small and very decorative they have always been looked upon as something precious, even if out of order. Unlike Germany, where the guild laws forbade the use of precious metals by clockmakers, the French made full use of silver and even gold in their table-clock cases. As might be expected the majority of these have been broken up for their valuable metal content, consequently the existing clocks give a very unbalanced picture of early clockmaking in France.

Plate 25 – The hexagonal clock was the most popular type during the sixteenth century. The trains are mounted one above the other in the case which is designed as a miniature tower with columns at each corner and surmounted by a pierced dome housing the bell. The movements of these clocks are equally architectural: the plates or 'floors' of the movement are supported by pillars at each corner. The movement, often standing on squat feet, is inserted into the case from below and held in position by the tightly-fitting base. The clock is also wound from below which means that the going fusée arbor on the top floor extends down to the bottom of the case. Similarly, the bell hammer has to be extended from the striking train mounted beneath up into the dome where the bell is mounted. The dial is always a part of the movement and appears through an aperture in the case.

French Renaissance clocks do not display quite the same grandeur or variety as their German counterparts until the end of the sixteenth century when new types, inspired by German designs, were adopted It is interesting to notice that the shape of the case of Renaissance clocks is determined by the construction of the movement – the two parts are inseparably related. Only later in the seventeenth century does the case become independent from the shape of the movement.

18. TWO TIER PLATED MOVEMENT OF SIXTEENTH-CENTURY TABLE CLOCKS. THE TOP PLATE IS PINNED ON WHILST THE BOTTOM PLATE IS REMOVED BY UNSCREWING THE FEET

During the period 1590 to 1610 the hexagonal shape almost disappeared, to be replaced by the recently-introduced square form. The architectural details of these square cases are less pronounced than on the former hexagonal ones. The four sides were often exquisitely engraved with foliage and flowers. Within France were numerous clockmaking centres, including Blois, Paris, Lyons, Marseilles, Abbeville and Autun. Each major centre had its own craft guilds.

The Paris Guilds

The Paris Guild of Clockmakers had its statutes changed a number of times between its formation in 1544 and 1691 when, in Louis XIV reign, its laws were rewritten. An apprentice was bound for eight years, although he could spend these years under more than one master. A master was allowed only one apprentice, although he could have numerous assistants. The laws were rather restrictive, allowing seventy-two qualified members of the Guild at any one time, and sons of established members were given special privileges.

Each craft had its own guild, cabinet-makers, gilders, founders, engravers, enamellers and so on. This resulted in perhaps half a dozen workshops working on or producing parts for one clock. Inevitably this caused friction between the various groups of craftsmen; arguments even arose from deciding who should transport a piece from one workshop to another. Variations in quality between constituent parts of a case can sometimes be detected.

Certain groups of craftsmen had the opportunity to streamline their production because they were free of the laws of the guilds and worked in districts controlled by the church or the king. These craftsmen could have as large a workshop and as many apprentices as they could manage. Within the Louvre were lodged many of the most distinguished craftsmen, including cabinet-makers and clockmakers working wholly or partly for the king.

Louis XIII and XIV

The seventeenth century saw a dramatic decline in clock production as the fashion for carrying watches on the person increased. The clocks of this period display wonderful quality, which probably reflected the precise and decorative work required in the making of watches.

By 1653 when Louis XIV came to the throne, the French clockmaking industry was dead. This explains why the early French pendulum clocks were such faithful copies of Dutch ones. For the first time clocks were housed in wooden cases whose size and shape were not strictly dictated by that of the movement. The pendulum clock was such a great improvement in accuracy that clocks once more became fashionable, and Paris now became firmly established as the centre of the French clockmaking industry.

The early pendulum clocks were known as *Pendules Religeuse* because their black ebony veneer gave them such a sombre appearance. Such a modest-looking clock could hardly satisfy for long the requirements of the aristocracy who, under the leadership of Louis XIV, were furnishing their houses in the most elaborate style based loosely on classical forms. The development of the Religeuse into a highly decorative article designed to fit in with the elaborate bronze mounted and inlaid furniture was rapid and predictable.

By the 1670s the square, box-like case had become embellished with baroque columns or pillasters at the corners, an elaborate entablature supported a shallow dome top surmounted with gilt finials. The veneer was usually tortoiseshell inlaid with pewter lines and foliage. The square dial aperture was now arch-topped and below the chaptering was often a figure of Father Time or some other allegorical figure in cast and gilt bronze. In the 1690s enamel plaques for each hour numeral were introduced. The minutes were still engraved around the edge of the dial. By the end of the century the lower portion of the dial was left open, except perhaps for a figure or name plaque and the inlaid interior of the clock could be seen.

Plate *26* – This is an elaborate *Pendule Religeuse* of the late seventeenth century. The wooden case is inlaid with tortoiseshell, brass and a white metal, most probably pewter. The shaped apron below the dial was a common feature of French pendulum clocks at this early date. The movement has a plain back plate engraved with the maker's name. The pendulum is suspended between cycloidal cheeks. Both going and striking trains have going barrels. As in the early

Dutch pendulum clock seen in plate 16, the striking, lifting and locking detent arbors have pierced steel 'gates' which are purely decorative.

The Royal manufactory at the Gobelin's on the outskirts of Paris was the birth-place of the Louis XIV style. It was set up in 1667 under the control of Le Brun, who employed not only French craftsmen, but also Flemish and Italians skilled in metal inlaying and tapestry. Here the classical baroque style matured, and no expense was spared to produce the very best of everything for the King's palace at Versailles.

During the last decade of the seventeenth century André Charles Boulle (1642–1732) was to become one of the most influential of cabinet-makers. In collaboration with Jean Berain he made magnificent pieces of inlaid furniture with marquetry of tortoiseshell and brass, pewter, silver, mother-of-pearl and numerous other materials. The designs are of linear arabesques combined with scrolling leafy foliage from which emerge grotesques and mythological creatures. The cast metal mounts on Boulle's own work tend to be secondary to the form of the piece and serve to enhance the inlay work.

During the first years of the eighteenth century the pedestal clock became very popular. The mounting of a spring-driven clock on a matching pedestal produced a very impressive piece of furniture. Drawings attributed to Oppendard exist showing weight-driven longcase clocks of about 1720, and some examples survive from as early as 1680 but they are most uncommon. At no period in French history was the weight-driven longcase clock produced in large numbers.

Plate 27 – A pedestal clock by Mynuel of Paris (1694–1750). The spring-driven movement sounds 'ting-tang' quarter-hours and is contained in a gilt bronze case with brass and dark brown tortoiseshell inlay. The bronze dial is finely chased and each hour numeral consists of a separate enamel plaque. The hands are of blued steel. The dial no longer fills the door aperture, and the inlaid and bronze mounted interior can be seen through the glass panel below the dial.

This is a clock of Boulle's period and it will be noticed that the decoration is always symmetrical. The motifs in use at this period include masks, shells, goats' heads, rearing seahorses, allegorical figures, lions' paws and the inevitable acanthus leaves. The inlay work of the late seventeenth and early eighteenth centuries is always of outstanding quality: the pieces fit perfectly and show no sign of the thickness of a saw cut. The metal inlay is always engraved.

Plate 28 – An early example of a cartel clock (from the Italian *cartela*, a bracket). The cartel clock, normally of gilt bronze, hangs on the wall and can range in size from 30 cm to 1·5 m (1 ft to 5 ft) in height. This clock was made by J. Thuret of Paris who was clock-maker to the king from 1694 to 1712, as his father had been before him. The design is perfectly symmetrical, incorporating festoons of flowers and rams' heads. The bronze case, basically of lyre form, contains a dial with enamelled plaques for the hours with the figures in blue. The hands at this period were almost a standard design and were of steel. Parts of the case are burnished, while others are left as a contrasting light matt gilt.

During the early eighteenth century a new feeling in furniture design was emerging. The weight of Louis XIV gave way to a freer and lighter style and for the first time asymmetrical designs appeared, especially in cartel clocks. The waisted shape became almost universal for bracket clocks, many of which still survive, together with their matching brackets. By about 1715–20 the enamelled dial centre was introduced. Throughout the century clock movements became more standardised. The bell was now often mounted on the back plate of the drum-shaped movement, since an increasing number of bronze cases now being made had restricted space for the movement. This period is rich in eminent craftsmen. Cressent, Caffieri, Meisonnier and Gaudreau were all men of creative genius, who made clock cases that were often superb pieces of sculpture in their own right.

Louis XV
Louis XV reigned from 1723 to 1774 and during these years styles changed dramatically. This period saw the rococo style come and go, being replaced by a much purer classical style than that of Louis XIV. The rococo is often thought of as a style in its own right, but strictly it is the last phase of the baroque style. There is no break in the

development of styles from Louis XIV to the mid-eighteenth century as there is between the rococo and the neoclassicism which followed. Rococo designs combine abstract curves and scrolls with shell- and coral-like shapes, as well as flowers and leaves and, later, Chinese and Gothic motifs.

One of the most popular types of clock was the waisted bracket clock. At first it was veneered with tortoiseshell and brass inlay with gilt mounts. Later examples are sometimes veneered in brightly coloured horn, and sometimes inlaid with flowers in contrasting colours. Others were lacquered and painted with flowers while some of the most superb are of bronze.

Plate 29 – An ornate rococo waisted bracket clock with its original wall bracket. The flat, one-piece enamelled dial is signed 'F. Lownoy A Paris' while the case is signed 'F. Goyer and J M E'. The wooden case is veneered with green shell inlaid with engraved brass flowers, mostly carnations. This piece is about 91 cm (3 ft) high, including the bracket.

Plate 30 – A small ormolu bracket clock, the movement by Stollewoik of Paris, who was master in 1746. This piece stands less than 30 cm (1 ft) high, and a cherub plays the pipes above the enamelled dial. This kind of case was to be copied extensively in England by some leading makers of the early nineteenth century.

When a clock with a particularly complex movement was required, it usually took the form of a tall clock. Very often it was made to look rather like a bracket clock on a pedestal, although it was in fact weight-driven. Rococo tall clocks are usually of exotic woods like kingwood, or inlaid with contrasting woods in delicate leafy designs. Invariably they are mounted with bronze. The designs of tall clocks are not always so successful or pleasing as the majority of bracket and cartel clocks, even though made by eminent cabinet-makers. From the horologist's viewpoint, however, tall clocks are among the most interesting. The movements are usually by leading makers and invariably have interesting escapements and other complicated features.

It was not uncommon for clocks to be incorporated effectively within pieces of furniture. Such great *ebonistes* as Nicholas Pineau,

56

Van Risen Burgh and Jacques Dubois made cabinets, desks and over-mantles in which clocks were set. The latter two craftsmen were also well-known for their lacquered furniture. As in England the craze for oriental decoration was long-lived. Panels of true Chinese and Japanese lacquer, usually of dark brown or black, were cut out of screens and fitted into cabinets and commodes. The French lacquer sometimes imitated oriental lacquer very closely, especially when a dark ground colour was used; however very brightly coloured pieces were also popular.

Oriental objects were sometimes included in animal clocks and the figures of a bull, elephant or horse supporting the clock may be of oriental porcelain. The animals of the French rococo may be of porcelain, or gilt or patinated bronze. The clock may be surmounted by a little figure of a Chinaman, a much-loved figure of rococo ornament.

The continuing search for new materials is reflected by the intro-duction of cases made wholly of porcelain. Such cases were somewhat impractical. Fitting a comparatively heavy movement into a fragile case is not easy. They can display wonderful intricacy, sometimes with branches of bronze wire supporting flowers and leaves. Invariably they stood on scrolled bronze bases.

Plate 31 – This beautiful porcelain case from the Meissen factory contains a movement by Etienne Lenoir of Paris. Below the dial emerges the winged torso of Father Time, while the clock is sur-mounted by a figure of Plenty, her basket overflowing with flowers.

The primary function of this piece as a clock is still quite evident, but some porcelain cases become a riot of flowers, figures and branches, making the clock dial look quite insignificant. Such pieces sometimes contain only a watch movement and are of little horo-logical interest.

The lyre clock is a type associated particularly with the reign of Louis XVI (1774–89). It incorporates marble, onyx or porcelain with bronze to produce what must surely be one of the most beautiful of clock forms.

Plate 32 – A fine example of a lyre clock by Lenoir of Paris, delicately combining cream marble with gilt mounts. The pendulum

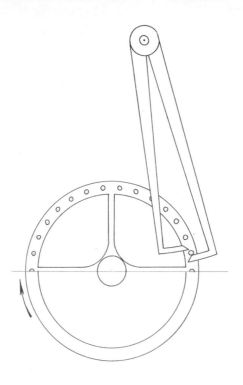

19. PIN WHEEL ESCAPEMENT. A FORM OF DEAD BEAT ESCAPEMENT INVENTED
BY AMANT IN 1749 AND USED IN FRENCH REGULATORS AND TURRET
CLOCKS

is formed by the ring of paste brilliants which encircles the prettily
enamelled dial. The pendulum rod is in the form of the strings of a
lyre, arranged as on a gridiron compensating pendulum.

Plate 33 – An important Louis XVI longcase regulator. The ebony
case has gilt bronze mouldings and restrained mounts, and gives a
false impression of being tapered. The enamelled dial is signed
Ferdinand Berthoud. A calendar disk is visible through an aperture
above the figure twelve. The steel pointer shows the equation of time,
that is, how much faster or slower solar time is than mean time.

Within the trunk door is an aperture containing a barometer. The massive gridiron pendulum is supported from an equally massive bracket fixed to the back board. The clock has count wheel striking, and stands about 2·2 m (7 ft 6 in) high.

At no other time had France possessed so many great clockmakers. Berthoud, Janvier, Lepaute, Robin and the greatest of them all, Breguet, were all men of genius who raised the industry to its greatest heights. Encouraged by Louis XVI, who took a personal interest in horological matters, the very first horological school was formed in 1786. Unfortunately it was a short-lived venture, since only three years elapsed before the Revolution.

Provincial Clockmaking
Paris had long been the only great centre of clockmaking in France, but mention must be made of the type of clock traditionally made in the Morbier area of the French Jura. The Comtoise clock, as it is known, was first made during the eighteenth century and (like those of the Black Forest) was made to the same design from one generation to the next. The weight-driven movements are made of iron and brass in the 4-poster manner. The pendulum hangs at the front of the movement and operates either an anchor escapement, or a verge when the crown wheel is mounted upside down. A unique system of rack striking is used which is often arranged to sound the last hour again two minutes after the hour. The fly on the striking train consists of four vanes instead of the usual two. The movements which are of 8-day duration, and occasionally of a month's duration, have iron doors to the sides and can be used as wall clocks or fitted into a tall case.

Plate 34a – This beautiful Comtoise longcase clock is signed on the enamelled dial 'Bailly A. Prémery'. The dial has a thin pressed brass surround of baroque scrolls and festoons of fruit and foliage. The lyre-shaped case follows that of the pendulum, and the decoration on the case is not inlaid but painted. The faked walnut graining is painted in lines of contrasting colours around the edges of the case.

Plate 34b – A Comtoise clock used as a wall clock.

The Neoclassic Period·

A curious situation arose in the second half of the eighteenth century: at the height of the rococo the classical style reappeared. This was a very different classicism to that of Louis XIV. It was a rebellion against the extravagances of the rococo and arose from a desire to find a new basis of simplicity and rationality. Laugier's *Essay on Architecture* of 1753 praises classical architecture as an economic expression of man's basic need for shelter. The Pantheon in Paris, designed by Souflot and begun in 1757, was the first truly neoclassical building in Paris. The neoclassical style emphasised the correct use of the orders, and the furniture of the period is linear, with decoration in low relief applied to the flat surfaces.

Clock cases in the new style were based on architecture. The clock might be set into a column of marble or porcelain or made as the pedestal for a small urn. The Sèvres factory produced porcelain vases of classical design into which clock movements were set. The chapter ring sometimes took the form of a horizontal band round the rim of the vase. The hours and minutes rotated past a fixed pointer. Figures from classical mythology also formed major parts of the case designs.

The Revolution of 1789 greatly disrupted the clockmaking and cabinet-making industries. Without the patronage of the aristocracy, few could carry on a successful business. However, the Directoire, formed in 1795, brought a stable government and in 1797 commerce was stimulated by the first of many industrial exhibitions held in Paris. The craft guilds had been dissolved in 1791 which meant that standards could be allowed to fall, while it had the advantage that makers could form businesses incorporating every branch of manufacture.

It was also a time of wonderful archaeological discoveries in Greece and Italy and this stimulated an academic interest in classical architecture and interior decoration. Many designers advocated the use of strict classical forms, a move led by such men as George Jacob, Percier and Fontaine and the artist David, who later became court painter to Napoleon.

Napoleon became Emperor in 1804 and saw himself as the head of a vast empire which would include the ancient Roman Empire. Along with the armies he took to Egypt went artists, designers and antiquarians who collected material at first hand. As a result, Empire furniture displays a mixture of classical and Egyptian forms.

Plate 35 – An Empire period mantel clock of about 1810 made in Paris. The drum-shaped striking movement has an enamelled dial with Breguet-style hands. A very rich effect is achieved by the application of the gilt reliefs on a coloured background. The use of individual motifs in low relief is typical of Empire decoration. An exciting contrast is made between the clock case and the boudoir scene which surmounts it.

Something must now be said of France's most gifted maker, Abraham Louis Breguet, who was born in 1742 near Neuchâtel, the great watchmaking centre of Switzerland. Nothing is known of his early career in Switzerland, but by 1787 he was making fine watches with lever escapements in Paris. All his work has a distinctive character and superb finish. He introduced many improvements for watches, one of the most important being a system of shock-proofing for the balance staff pivots. He made clocks and watches with perpetual calendars which allowed for the short months and for leap years. He also made a number of calendar clocks in silver cases which were designed for travelling. They are fitted with watch escapements mounted on the back-plate. These clocks were much copied. After his death in 1823 the business was carried on by his son and subsequently by his grandson.

Plate 36 – The influence of the Empire style continued well into the mid-nineteenth century. This 4-pillar clock supporting a heavy entablature was made in the 1830s, but the style originated in the 1800s. Although the form of the clock is very severe, the inlay and decorative pendulum and dial surround heralds the return of the fussy and sometimes over-elaborate designs of the later nineteenth century.

Mass Production
The introduction of steam-powered machinery led to great advances in production methods. French movements which had become

standardised in the eighteenth century were now produced in very large numbers and put into a wide range of cases. It was a period when designers sought novelty rather than elegance.

Plate 37a and b – This picture clock reflects the growing interest in the Gothic which was evident by the 1830s. Behind the canvas, and mounted within a shallow box, is a quarter-striking ting-tang movement, the dial of which appears through a hole in the canvas. The movement is identical to thousands of others made throughout the century and is stamped GANCHY. The hour is struck on the larger of the two gongs. The clock's silk suspension is regulated by the small arbor which protrudes through the top of the front plate.

No. 5536.

Size, 12 × 6 ... ... £6

No. 5537.

Size, 19 × 10 ... ... £12.

Smaller ... ... £8 8s.

20. BUHL CLOCKS FOR DINING ROOM, DRAWING ROOM OR BOUDOIR. A PLATE FROM THE CATALOGUE OF J. W. BENSON LTD., c. 1890

Plate 38 – A novelty clock known as a *Mysterieuse*, dating from the second half of the nineteenth century. The drum-shaped striking movement is contained in the marble base and the bronzed spelter figure holding the pendulum stands on a base connected indirectly to the escapement. The base rotates through a minute angle to keep the pendulum in motion. The glass pendulum bob is signed 'S. D. McKellen, Paris'. Some *Mysterieuse* clocks have the movement in the pendulum bob.

In the 1880s a great many cheap reproductions of earlier styles were introduced. The accompanying photograph shows a page from the catalogue of Bensons' of Ludgate Hill, London, advertising 'Buhl' bracket clocks in wooden cases with brass mounts. Earlier examples

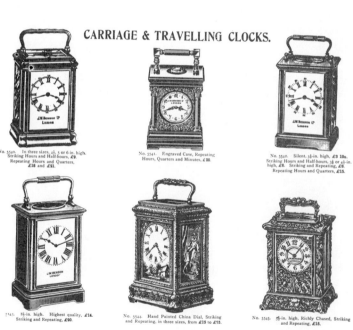

CARRIAGE & TRAVELLING CLOCKS.

No. 5540. In three sizes, 4½, 5 or 6-in. high. Striking Hours and Half-hours, £9. Repeating Hours and Quarters, £18 and £21.

No. 5541. Engraved Case, Repeating Hours, Quarters and Minutes, £20.

No. 5542. Silent, 3½-in. high, £3 10s. Striking Hours and Half-hours, 3½ or 4½-in. high, £6. Striking and Repeating, £8. Repeating Hours and Quarters, £15.

No. 5543. 8½-in. high. Highest quality, £16. Striking and Repeating, £20.

No. 5544. Hand Painted China Dial, Striking and Repeating, in three sizes, from £15 to £18.

No. 5545. 5½-in. high, Richly Chased, Striking and Repeating, £18.

21. SELECTION OF FRENCH CARRIAGE CLOCKS FROM THE CATALOGUE OF J. W. BENSON LTD., *c.* 1890

63

have brass and tortoiseshell inlay, but the quality bears no comparison with eighteenth-century work.

The same catalogue illustrates a wide range of carriage clocks, but although they display Bensons' name they are entirely of French manufacture.

Plate 39 – Another novelty clock, a carriage clock surmounted by an animated bird which can be made to twitter and flap its wings. The subsidiary dial is for setting the alarm. Clocks intended to be used as travelling clocks were sold with close fitting wooden cases covered with leather to protect them during the journey. They were certainly never intended for use in a carriage as the English name implies.

Makers such as Breguet had produced carriage clocks as early as 1810, but their large-scale production did not commence till the 1840s–1850s and it continued unchanged well into the present century. The movements were made in various provincial towns, such as Lyons and St Nicholas, and were sent to the numerous Paris workshops to be finished to the required standard. From these workshops they would be sent to the retailer whose name would appear on the dial. The cases would be ordered from specialist case makers, as were the platform watch-type escapements which were made by craftsmen working in towns on the Swiss border.

Plate 40a – Nowhere is the continuing influence of neoclassicism more evident than in the heavy marble mantle clocks of the late nineteenth century. This green onyx and brass example is unusually decorative for such clocks. The design of the case is surely inspired by the Parthenon.

The majority of so-called black marble cases are actually made of polished slate and are cemented together with a compound of Russian tallow, brick dust and resin. Not all marble clocks are of mediocre quality. Brocot (d. 1878) made some fine calendar clocks with moon phase dials and other complicated refinements.

Plate 40b – A small, travelling alarm clock of the early twentieth century complete with its tightly-fitting turned wooden box and instruction label (fig. 23). The clock is unusual in that it is controlled by a pendulum only 5 cm (2 in) long. The long dial pointer sets the alarm. The maker's name, T. Maurel, is engraved on the back cover

1   An iron Gothic chamber clock with verge escapement and foliot suspended by a thread.
This clock strikes the hours and has an alarm.

2 A gilt brass cased Augsburg table clock or tabernacle clock, early 17th century. It has been converted to a pendulum control from a balance wheel. The silver dials retain traces of the original coloured enamel in the deep engraving.

3a An anonymous drum-shaped table clock of about 1580. The little knobs at each hour are for feeling the time in the dark.

3b A hexagonal brass table clock of about 1700 by Mayer of Augsburg. Similar clocks are found bearing English makers' names at this period.

4 An early 17th-century table clock incorporating animated figures. The Negro who points to the hour with his spear moves his head when the hour is struck and the dog appears to run at his feet.

5 Another clock incorporating an animated figure. The griffon holding the dial flaps its wings and moves its beak as the hour is struck.

6 An Austrian fruitwood bracket clock signed on the chapter ring, 'Ge. Preisacher, Clostemenburg'. In the arch is a central calendar dial and two subsidiary dials for the strike/silent and chime/silent. In the centre of the backplate is a large engraved cartouche.

7   A beautiful pale yellow lacquered bracket clock by Adalbertus Hockenadl of the late 18th
    century. It stands 21 in. (53 cm) high, and its 40 hour movement chimes the quarter hours
    on eight bells.

8 A Neuchâteloise or Swiss bracket clock from the Neuchâtel region. This early 19th-century example has a rosewood brass inlaid case and sits upon an integral bracket on the wall. The movement has *grande sonnerie* quarter striking.

9 A Biedermeier period mantel clock of about 1825, 18 in. (46 cm) high, signed 'Niederlags Compagnie, in Wien'. It has a quarter chiming movement and the pendulum regulation square can be seen over the figure 12.

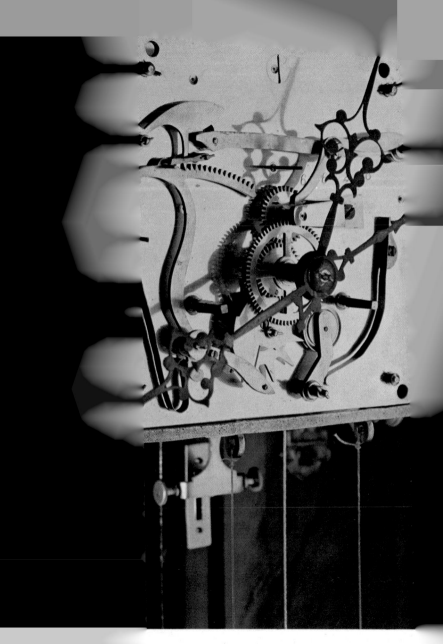

ovement from a late 19th-century Vienna regulator, showing
d on all Austrian clocks of the 19th century.

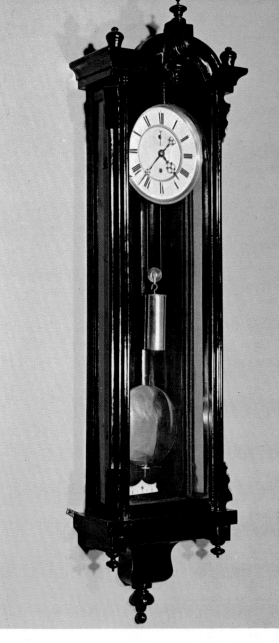

11a   A longcase Vienna regulator chiming the quarters. The fine and severe design of the case is typical of early 19th-century Vienna regulators.

11b   A later 19th-century Vienna regulator. The case is becoming more fussy with a cresting and finials.

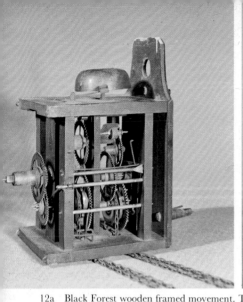

12a   Black Forest wooden framed movement. The wooden arbors are often painted silver to imitate steel.

12b   Traditional Black Forest shield dial.

12c   An early cuckoo clock with enamelled dial.

12d   Spring driven wall clock with wooden framed movement.

13a   Three mass produced Black Forest shelf clocks.

13b   Late nineteenth-century cuckoo clock.

13c   Movement of a simple mass produced cuckoo clock showing the bellows.

14 The so-called postman's alarm. The final development of the Black Forest clock with wooden plates. This one was retailed in 1914.

15 Early Haagse clock movement, signed 'J. Van Ceulen, Hague'. The dial is
case to allow easy access to the movement.

16   The Haagse clock to which the movement in Plate 15 belongs. The plain ebony-veneered case has delicate mouldings and is architectural in style. The skeleton chapter ring and Father Time are mounted on a velvet-covered dial plate.

A magnificent silver and gilt cased clock by Adriaen Van den Bergh of The Hague, late 17th century. A masterpiece of decorative metalwork.

18 A striking and alarm bracket clock in an ebonised case by Roger Dunster of Amsterdam, of about 1745. A Dutch example of an English style. The central alarm disk is typically Dutch, rarely found on similar English clocks.

19 Two Zaanse clocks; that on the left is signed 'Groot, 1725', has double striking and strikes once at the quarters. The clock on the right has a painted dial plate.

20 A Friesland Stoel clock of the 18th century. This alarm clock has a verge escapement but does not strike the hours. Clocks with similar movements were made as early as the mid-17th century and may have inspired the design of Japanese 'lantern' clocks.

21 A Staart clock, probably late 18th century. The nicely painted dial has a complicated automaton scene below the chapter ring. The windmill sails turn with the escape wheel whilst the ship and the fisherman's rod move with the swing of the pendulum.

22   The 30 hour movement of Plate 21 has well turned corner posts and hammer arbor. It has an anchor escapement and strikes the hours on the large bell and again at half past on the small bell.

23a A magnificent mulberry-veneered and ebony-moulded long case clock by Roger Dunster of Amsterdam, *c.* 1760. The musical movement plays twelve tunes on a massive pin barrel mounted across the backplate.

23b A walnut-veneered longcase clock by Van Brussel of Amsterdam. It has a buttressed *bombe* base and fine wooden frets to the front and sides of the hood.

24   A musical longcase movement of the mid-18th century by F. Bavius of Leeuwarden. The
lever to select the tunes can be seen on the barrel arbor to the left. The fly for regulating
the musical train can be seen on the back plate with its adjustable vanes.

25   A 16th-century hexagonal French table clock, less than 6 in. (15 cm) high, designed like a tower with pillasters at each corner. The dial seems very deeply set since it is fixed to the movement rather than the case. Through the side windows can be seen the two tier movement. This clock may originally have stood on a moulded wooden plinth.

26 A late 17th-century *Religeuse* clock, a development of the Dutch Haagse clock. The silk
pendulum suspension hangs between cycloidal cheeks. The bell is mounted in the dome.
The case is covered in marquetry of tortoise-shell, brass and pewter. Note the shaped
apron below the dial.

27 An important Boulle marquetry pedestal clock. The movement made by Mynuel of Paris, sounds ting-tang quarter hours. The case may be from C. A. Boulle's own workshop.

28   An early 18th-century bronze-cased cartel clock by J. Thuret of Paris (1694-1712). A fine example of the symmetrical baroque ornamentation of the Louis XIV period.

A decorative rococo clock on its matching bracket. The movement is by Lournoy of Paris. The wooden case veneered with green-tinted shell is inlaid with brass and is signed by F. Goyer and stamped 'J.M.E.'

30 A small ormolu bracket or mantel clock. The word ormolu means ground gold and may
be used to describe any gold plated metal. The movement with silk suspension and
numbered countwheel is by Stollewerk of Paris (c 1740-70).

31 A Louis XV mantel clock. The gilded bronze and Meissen porcelain case contains a Paris
made movement.

32　A fine lyre clock by Lenoir of Paris. The pendulum bob is formed by the ring of paste brilliants which encircles the dial. The restrained elegance of this clock is characteristic of the Louis XVI period at its best.

33 A very fine Louis XVI long-case weight-driven regulator of ebony. The precision movement is signed 'Ferdinand Berthoud'. A barometer is mounted in the trunk.

34a A Comtoise clock used as a wall clock. The enamel dial has a thin *repoussé* brass surround and the movement is contained within iron dust covers.

34b A fine Comtoise longcase clock signed 'Bailly a Prémery'. The surface of the case is painted.

35 An Empire period mantel clock on top of which is a delicate boudoir scene. The clock is contained under a glass dome.

36   A four pillar or pediment clock of the 1830's in rosewood with gilt mouldings.

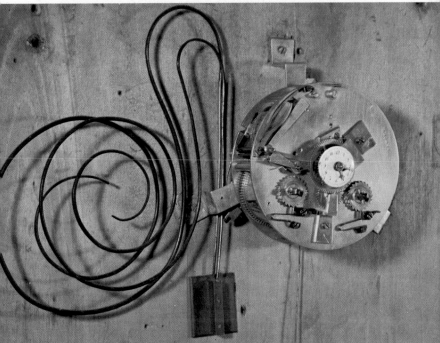

37 A 19th-century picture clock and its movement. The picture is in oils on canvas and the ting-tang quarter striking movement is contained within a shallow box behind the frame.

38. A novelty clock known as a *Mysterieuse*. The pendulum bob is signed in gilt lettering 'S. D. McKellan, Paris'.

39 A 19th-century brass carriage clock surmounted by an automated singing bird in a cage.

40a   A green marble mantel clock of the late 19th century.

40b   A travelling alarm clock of the early 20th century complete with its protective box.

41 The Bulle electric clock designed by Fauvre-Bulle. An early example of electrically driven domestic clocks.

42   An early Atmos clock. Invented by J. E. Reutter in Paris in 1913, it uses the constant changes in atmospheric temperature to keep the mainspring fully wound.

43 A mid-17-century table clock by David Bouquet of London. The square movement is shown standing on its side. The striking train going barrel is finely pierced.

44 An English lantern clock made wholly of iron except for the brass chapter ring and hand. The front fret bears the signature 'John Holloway at Lavington 1611'. Apart from the rather unusual hexagonal corner columns this clock is identical to later brass lantern clocks.

45a   A brass lantern clock signed by Hercules Hastings of Burford contained in a heavy oak case with side doors to the hood.

45b   A small ebony veneered long case clock by Ahaseurus Fromanteel with verge escapement and short pendulum of about 1665.

46   A fine silver-mounted quarter-repeating bracket clock of veneered ebony made by Thomas Herbert of London, clockmaker to the King. He worked from 1676 to 1708.

47 A well engraved back plate from a bracket clock of about 1715 made by James
    Blackborow. Notice the catch to the rear right of the dial which when turned secures the
    clock in the case. The clock repeats the quarter hours at will on six bells.

48a   A very decorative late 17th-century marquetry longcase clock by Daniel Quare. Above the dial is a *repoussé* brass frieze. The hour hand is particularly finely pierced. Notice the alternate use of ebony and walnut for the mouldings.

48b   A magnificent early 18th-century lacquered longcase clock signed 'Marwick Londini', with its original domed top and silvered finials intact.

49   An English eight-day longcase clock movement of about 1720 by Windmills, showing the rack striking work normally hidden by the dial. The English longcase clock movement remained unchanged for the next 150 years except for decorative details.

50   A bracket clock by Joseph Windmills of London made especially for the German market where the use of mirror glass on furniture was very fashionable at this period. The simple arch top to the case was not usual on English bracket clocks but avoided having to make a complicated dome in glass. This clock can be dated about 1715-1720.

51 A rare example of a bracket clock made to one of Thomas Chippendale's designs in the mid-18th century. The beautiful case of carved mahogany contains a movement by Archambo and Marchant of London. The original verge escapement has been converted to anchor. The clock stands about 2 ft. (61 cm) high.

52 A London made gilt wood cartel clock with verge escapement signed 'Wintmills' of about
    1775. An English example of a French type.

53   A very beautiful Chelsea porcelain flower clock containing a watch movement. The dial is about 1½ in. (3.75 cm) in diameter. An almost identical piece containing a movement by John Fladgate exists. This case would originally have been mounted upon a scrolling ormolu stand.

54   A late 18th-century gilt metal case made by Matthew Boulton of Birmingham after a
design by Sir William Chambers. The movement is by Eardley Norton and the dial was
enamelled by Weston of Smithfields.

55 An ebonised bracket clock made for the Turkish market in the 1790's by Recordon and Dupont. The painted dial bears Turkish numerals and in the arch are strike/silent and pendulum regulation dials. The elaborate side frets and dome are typical of clocks exported to the Near East.

56   A late 18th-century ebonised bell-top bracket clock with a Bilston enamel dial.

57 A bracket clock movement typical of early 19th-century English work. The cord is for pull repeat. The strike/silent lever can be seen in front of the bell.

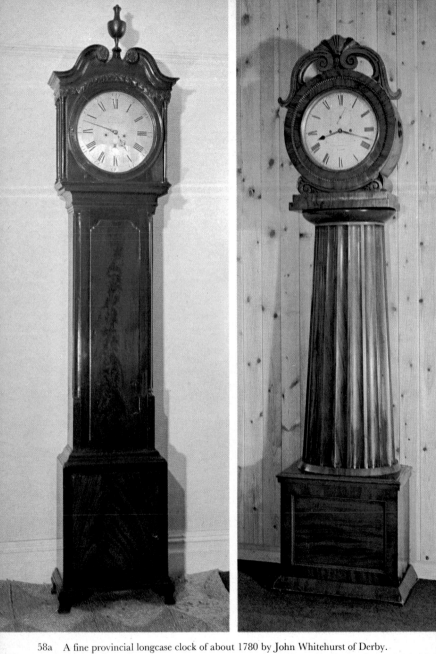

58a   A fine provincial longcase clock of about 1780 by John Whitehurst of Derby.

58b   A unique Scottish longcase clock designed as a fluted Doric column. The cresting may or
may not be original.

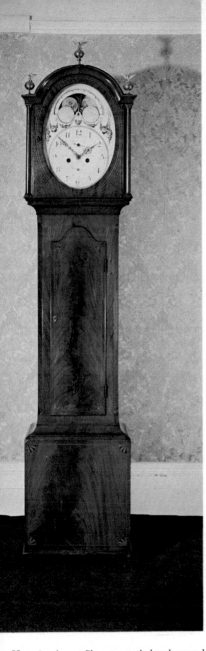

59a   An elegant Sheraton period mahogany longcase clock. The oval painted dial contains a universal tidal dial signed 'Gowland of Blyth'.

59b   A small 8 in. (20 cm) dial wall clock. The eight day striking weight-driven movement is contained within tin dust covers and is fixed to the wall by a hook and spikes.

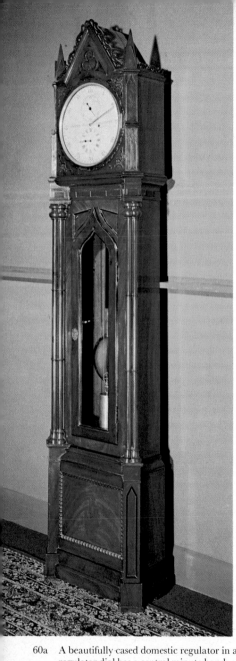

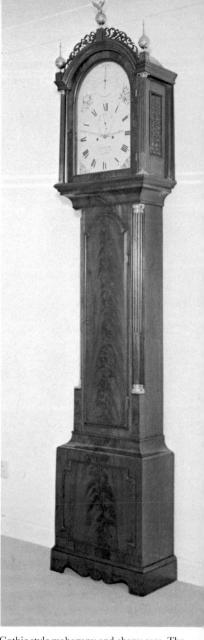

60a   A beautifully cased domestic regulator in a Gothic style mahogany and ebony case. The regulator dial has a central minute hand, a seconds dial below the figure 60 and the hour dial above the figure 30.

60b   A London mahogany longcase clock signed on the full arched painted dial and on the back plate by French, Royal Exchange, London. The hands are of brass *c* 1820.

An English dial clock. The wooden dial is signed 'Alcock and Wright' whilst the movement was actually made by Handley and Moore of London. The spade hands are of brass dating about 1800.

A painted iron dial wall clock by Barwise with a $\frac{1}{2}$-seconds pendulum encased within a figured mahogany trunk.

62 'Hope' style clock by Desbois & Wheeler of Gray's Inn Passage.

63   Chamfer top bracket clock of perfect proportions by D. & W. Morice, Cornhill.

64   Gothic style chiming clock by Viner and Co.

65   A high quality regulator. The silvered dial signed 'Tupman, London'.

66   A Victorian skeleton clock in the form of Lichfield Cathedral. Its glass dome is not shown in the photograph.

67a Mahogany cased tall clock by Isaac Doolittle of New Haven, Conn. of the mid-18th century.

67b Fine cherrywood-cased tall clock by Thomas Harland of Norwich. Conn. *c* 1790.

67c Thirty hour tall clock by Eli Terry in a cherry wood case of about 1800 with wooden movement and dial.

68   Pillar and scroll clock. 30 hour weight-driven wood movement made by Ephraim Downes for George Mitchell of Bristol Conn. *c.* 1827.

69a   Banjo clock by Simon Willard, Roxbury, Mass. of about 1820.

69b   Llyre clock by Samuel Abbot, Montpelier, Vermont, 1810. Brass eight day weight-driven movement.

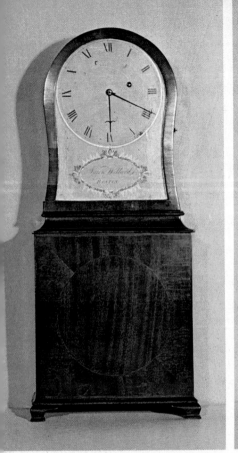

70a   Massachusetts shelf clock by Aaron Willard of Boston, Mass. It has an eight day brass weight-driven movement *c.* 1800.

70b   Wagon spring clock by Joseph Ives, Brooklyn, New York, *c.* 1825. Compare case style with that of the contemporary clock on Plate 62.

71 The works of a wagon spring clock. The system of levers amplifies the movement of the spring.

72 a & b   The dial and movement of a hanging wall clock made to one of Benjamin Franklin's designs.

72c   Thirty hour O.G. shelf clock. Brass weight-driven movement of the second half of 19th century.

72d   Eight day column shelf clock, after 1860, by Seth Thomas.

73a   Marbled wooden-cased mantel clock by the Waterbury Clock Co.

73b   Small alarm shelf clock by Seth Thomas.

73c   Steeple clock by Jerome of New Haven.

73d   *Fusée* movement by Jerome, *c.* 1853.

74a Mantel clock of cast iron imitating French clocks of the period.

74b 'Anglo' wall clock made for the British market.

74c A good quality four glass clock by the Ansonia Clock Co.

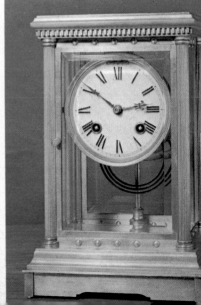

75a   A Japanese print showing in the background a lantern clock on its stand. Notice its height in relation to the seated figure.

75b   A Japanese painting on silk by Nishikawa Sukenobu (1671-1751) showing a lady winding up a lantern clock hanging from the wall.

75c   A 19th-century lantern clock on its wooden stand covered by an ornamental hood. The clock is controlled by a double foliot.

76 Two views of a Japane[se] bracket or table clock, o[ne] showing the clock in its ca[se] and the other showing t[he] back plate of the clock out [of] its case.

77 A small table clock about 5 in. (13 cm) wide with the front plate beautifully decorated with *cloisonné* enamel. The rotating dial shows hours and half-hours on adjustable plates. This clock is controlled by a bob pendulum and has a glazed wooden protective case not shown in the photograph.

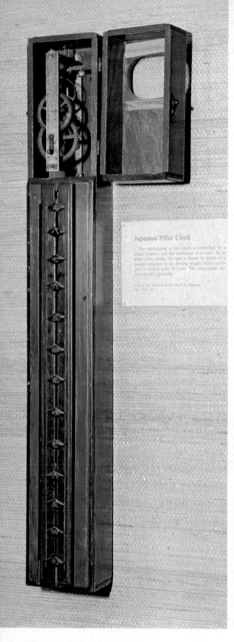

78a   An early pillar clock with an iron movement controlled by a foliot. Down the front of the case are the adjustable hour numerals.

78b   An elaborate pillar clock showing the hours on a graduated scale, the movement which has a very beautiful front plate is controlled by a balance wheel.

79 A rare inro clock $2\frac{1}{2}$ in. (7 cm) high. The tiny spring driven movement with a verge and balance wheel fits snugly into the inro case. A small pointer marks the hour which rotates past a hole in the case. The movement can be wound without removing it from its case.

80 A drum-shaped Chinese table clock with verge escapement and balance wheel. The Chinese hour characters are on an outer enamelled ring whilst the twenty-four European hours are engraved upon an inner brass ring. The clock also has an alarm mechanism. The decorative sides to the case depict the Pa Chi-Hsiang or eight Buddhist symbols.

22. PIN PALLET ESCAPEMENT INVENTED BY ACHILLE BROCOT OF PARIS (1817–1878) USING AGATE PALLETS

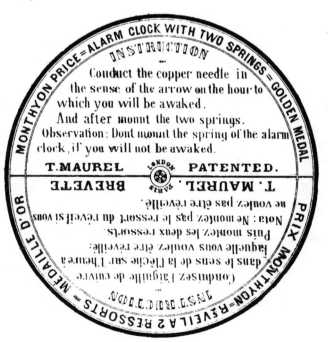

MONTHYON PRICE=ALARM CLOCK WITH TWO SPRINGS=GOLDEN MEDAL

INSTRUCTION

Conduct the copper needle in the sense of the arrow on the hour to which you will be awaked.

And after mount the two springs.

Observation: Dont mount the spring of the alarm clock, if you will not be awaked.

T. MAUREL   LONDON PARIS   **PATENTED.**

23. INSTRUCTION LABEL FROM THE TRAVELLING ALARM CLOCK SEEN IN PLATE 40b

of the case. This clock was a cheaper substitute for the heavy and more easily damaged carriage clock.

Twentieth-century Inventions

By the early nineteenth century the possibility of electrically-operated clocks was demonstrated by J. A. De Luc in France, F. Ronalds in England and by Professor Ramis in Munich. However it was another century before electric clocks were made economically for domestic use. The two most well-known were the Eureka clock and the Bulle clock. The principle of these clocks, however, had been developed by Alexander Bain in 1843.

Plate 41 – This is the Bulle clock designed by Fauvre-Bulle. On the end of the pendulum is a solenoid which encircles a consequent pole magnet. The clock is battery operated and receives an impulse to the pendulum in one direction only; the contact is made on one side only of the crutch-like lever, which engages with a silver pin on the pendulum. The actual swinging of the pendulum pushes the wheels of the clock round one tooth at a time. The delicate ratchet work can be seen within the dial centre and to its left can be seen the contact breaker. A number of different models were made, some housed in wooden mantel and wall cases, while others stood under a glass dome.

The Eureka clock works on the same principle, but instead of a pendulum it has a very heavy balance wheel running on glass roller bearings.

Plate 42 – The Atmos clock invented by J. E. Reutter of Paris in 1913. He used the constant changes in atmospheric pressure to wind the mainspring of a clock, but his idea was apparently not put into production at that time. The clock which was produced some years later makes use of temperature instead of pressure changes. A bellows within the drum-shaped cover behind the clock is filled with ethyl chloride which is highly sensitive to temperature changes. The movement is controlled by a heavy slow-moving temperature-compensated balance suspended on an invar strip. The dial of this example, probably made in the late 1930s, is signed 'ATMOS *pendule perpetuelle,* France'. The modern Atmos clock is made in Switzerland.

6

England

New Standards Introduced from the Continent

Henry VIII took a great interest in the arts and sciences, and was determined to make his palaces as sumptuous as those of his French contemporary Francis I. To achieve this he had to employ many craftsmen and artists from the Continent, who brought with them Renaissance ideas and designs. However the style was slow to mature, and shows a mixture of Gothic, Italian and Flemish features.

In 1517 the London apprentices rioted in protest against the number of foreign craftsmen in the city. A contemporary writer commented that 'the poore English artificers could skace get any livinge; and most of all the straungers were so proud that they disdained, mocked and oppressed the Englishmen'. They also 'much surpassed the Englishe in dexterity, industry and frugality'. But it was the standards introduced by these men, which the English adopted, that led to England's clockmaking supremacy by 1700. In the late sixteenth century English work, whether made by Englishmen or by French or Flemish craftsmen working in London, was very similar to work produced on the other side of the Channel. Table clocks had plated movements and can be compared with plate 25.

Plate 43a – A mid-seventeenth century square table clock by David Bouquet of London. This maker was a Frenchman free of the Blacksmith's Company in 1628, and was one of the first members of the Clockmakers Company on its incorporation in 1632. The 12-hour dial has a single hand and has 'touch pieces'. The pierced circles in the sides of the case are to let out the sound of the bell which is mounted in that corner.

Plate 43b – The movement of the Bouquet table clock. It is positioned to show the going train fusée, the hour bell and the striking train going barrel which is pierced and engraved. The balance wheel is pivoted in a pierced and engraved cock, the foot of which is similarly decorated. Below the balance lies the iron count-wheel. The stop work for the striking train is also pivoted beneath a beautifully decorated cock. The fusée set-up ratchet is on the right. The notched disks at opposite corners of the back plate are to secure the movement in its case.

Plate 44 – During the seventeenth century English clocks took on a recognisable national character as London became an important clockmaking centre. This clock owes little to continental types and is immediately recognisable as English. The use of iron in the framework is reminiscent of Gothic chamber clocks, while the classical Doric columns at the corners and the urn finials are typical of English lantern clocks. The name lantern clock may have arisen because of its loose resemblance to a lantern, but may also be a corruption of the old English word *latten* meaning brass in beaten sheet form.

Most lantern clocks were made to hang on the wall or to sit on a wooden bracket on the wall. After the introduction of the longcase clock some were made with free-standing cases, while in provincial areas open frameworks, usually of oak, were made to support them.

Plate 45a – A fine example of a late seventeenth-century brass lantern clock mounted in a panelled oak case. It has no central finial over the bell since this would not be seen through the hood aperture. This clock, which is signed by Hercules Hastings of Burford, was almost certainly made in the workshops of the famous Knibb family of Oxford and is fitted with a tic-tac escapement which spans only two teeth of the escape wheel. At the time the Knibbs were experimenting with the tic-tac escapement which it was thought would be more suited to a short pendulum than the recently invented anchor, although the action of the two is similar.

The Worshipful Company of Clockmakers
In 1631 Charles I granted the clockmakers of London a Charter of Incorporation for their own company. The Company, a descendant of the craft guilds, had wide powers over any clockmaker working within ten miles of the city. They made sure the work was of a high standard and their officers had the power to search workshops and order poor quality work to be destroyed.

An apprentice served seven years. He then had to spend two years as a journeyman and produce his 'masterpiece' before he could gain the 'freedom' of the Company. Not until a man became a Master Warden or Assistant of the Company could he take on more than one apprentice and then the maximum was only two at any one time.

The Golden Age of English Clockmaking
No other era of horological history has been so thoroughly researched as the first years of the pendulum clock. As soon as Huygens had produced his first pendulum clock, Ahaseurus Fromanteel, working in London, sent his son Johannes to work for Huygens. Johannes stayed in the Hague from September 1657 to May 1658, just long enough to learn about the new invention. By November the same year his father was advertising the first pendulum clocks to be made in England. Why Huygens apparently had no objection to the English learning of the pendulum at first hand is something of a mystery, especially as he tried several times to patent his invention in France as he had done in Holland. Fortunately there were no such restrictions in England and soon many makers had started making clocks with pendulums.

Under Charles II these makers introduced many improvements. The first spring-driven clocks made by Fromanteel were very closely based on Coster's work. There were no fusées, the dials were rectangular and hinged to the case to allow access to the movement attached to the rear of the dial. The cases were of ebony veneered oak, very plain in appearance and they could be used as table clocks or wall clocks. It is generally believed that it was common practice at this period to gild the brass plates and wheels, and blue the steel work of the movement. To blue the steel the pieces were laid in a tray of sand and evenly heated. As the temperature rose the steel changed from silver through yellow brown and eventually to blue, when it was quenched in oil. Not only does such treatment enhance the appearance of the movement but also protects it against rust. This practice, however, only lasted a few years – perhaps up to the 1670s.

Until that date both spring-and weight-driven clocks were fitted into ebony cases which followed very closely the architectural ideas of Palladio; all the mouldings, columns and proportions were in

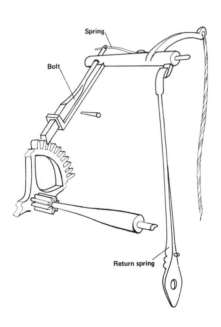

24. BOLT AND SHUTTER
MAINTAINING POWER
(SHUTTERS OMITTED)

accord with the classical principles which Sir Christopher Wren was also using on his great London churches.

Plate 45b – A longcase clock of about 1660–65 by Ahaseurus Fromanteel. It may, however, have started life as a wall clock, since it is unusual to find inverted finials below the hood moulding of a longcase, but it was certainly cased very shortly after it was made. The 8-day movement has a bob pendulum and verge escapement and, as is normal with very early longcase clocks, it also has bolt and shutter maintaining power. When a cord is pulled or a lever depressed the shutters which normally cover the winding squares are moved aside and at the same moment a sprung ratchet, the bolt, operates upon the centre wheel which keeps the going train in motion while the clock is being wound.

Around 1670 the anchor escapement was invented for use with the long pendulum which Dr Hook had demonstrated would improve timekeeping. Some makers used a 1·5 m (5 ft) $1\frac{1}{4}$ seconds beating pendulum, which was the longest a longcase clock could conveniently accommodate with the bob swinging in the base. The seconds pendulum, about a metre long, which enabled a dial showing exact seconds to be fitted, was soon universally adopted. However, the seconds pendulum could not be housed in the very narrow cases which had been made for the clocks with verge escapement and bob pendulum. At much the same time as the cases became wider to accommodate the seconds pendulum the architectural style of case went out of favour together with the use of ebony for longcase clocks.

An interesting description of a bracket clock of the 1660–70 period appeared in *The Postman* in the year 1700: 'Stolen from Mr Chute's house the upper end of Bedford Row. Near Grays Inn, on Saturday 29th June last, between 10 and 11 at night a large old heavy pendulum table clock made by Fromantle [sic] and his name engraven on the back plate, a little silver cherub's head at each corner of the dyal plate, fixt in an ebony case of about a foot square made in the form of a house.' It is interesting to note that a spring-driven clock was then known as a table clock.

On 24th June 1664 Samuel Pepys wrote in his diary that in the

Queen's bed chamber was 'nothing but some pretty pious pictures and books of devotion, and her holy water at her head as she sleeps with her clock by her bedside, wherein a lamp burns that tells her the time of night at any time'. This clock may well have been made by Edward East or Fromanteel. It could even be that Johannes Fromanteel had learnt the principle of the night clock while working in the Hague.

The first night clocks of this kind were made in Italy by the Campani brothers of Rome. English clocks have engraved and painted dials, the painting, Flemish in character, usually shows figures in landscape. In the upper portion of the dial is a semi-circular aperture divided into the quarter hours and minutes of one hour and across which pass each hour numeral in turn. The cut out quarters and hour numerals are illuminated from behind by an oil lamp mounted within the clock. Both longcase and table night clocks were made, but they constituted something of a fire risk and needed nightly attention to set the lamp. They were superseded by the pull quarter repeat mechanism which sounded the time to the nearest quarter of an hour on bells at the pull of a cord.

Plate 46 – A beautiful quarter repeating clock sounding the quarters at will on three bells. Only just over 30 cm (1 ft) high, it is suitable for carrying from one room to another. It was made c 1685 by Thomas Herbert who worked between 1676 and 1708 and was clockmaker to the King. The mounts on this clock are of solid silver as are the cherub head spandrels. The shallow dome or basket top had superseded the architectural top and by 1700 had become very elaborate.

At this period tortoiseshell was being increasingly used in England as a veneer for bracket clocks. When used as a veneer the shell, usually tinted red on the reverse and combined with silver or gilt mounts, gave a very rich effect. It was obtained from the Hawksbill turtle and the largest pieces were only 30–38 cm (12–15 in) in diameter. When heated it becomes pliable and can be moulded and stamped and retains its shape on cooling. It can also be welded together, thus increasing its thickness or area.

The French used tortoiseshell and various metals in marquetry.

This kind of inlay, made popular by C. A. Boulle, was also used on some clocks, longcase and bracket, by a number of leading makers in London. These clocks were probably made for continental customers and the inlay work may well have been carried out by French craftsmen in London. Other continental customers would order an English movement and have it cased up in France or Germany to suit their decorative schemes.

All kinds of exotic materials were used for bracket clock cases. Recently a bracket clock veneered completely in mother-of-pearl was discovered. Travelling clocks and miniature bracket clocks were often made with silver or gilt brass cases.

The back plate of a bracket clock presents a large area of brass which, on the architectural cased clock, is usually relieved only by the engraved signature of the maker. By 1675 back plates often display lively engraved tulip designs of a pronounced Dutch character.

Plate 47 – The back plate of a clock *c* 1720 by James Blackborow, of London. Here the large flowing tulips of the seventeenth century have developed into a tighter design of scrolling foliage and arabesques with a basket of flowers in the centre.

Perhaps the finest engraved designs were executed in the early eighteenth century. Among the foliage may be found birds, animals, cherubs, serpents, grotesque heads and often a shaped cartouche bearing the maker's name. Some of the best engraving was done by Frenchmen who were well known for their excellent work. The records of the Clockmakers Company show that a number of French craftsmen were admitted as brothers of the Company and described simply as engravers. Such men would work for a number of clockmakers. The engraved back plate in plate 47, for example, is identical in design and workmanship to another on a clock by the Royal clockmaker Thomas Cartwright.

Many of the decorative features introduced during the late seventeenth century can be traced back to Holland. Joseph Knibb, for instance, made bracket clocks with velvet-covered dial plates, silver hands and chapter rings. The Dutch mania for flowers, especially tulips, is reflected not only in back plate designs but in the engraving on lantern clocks and in the floral designs on marquetry cases.

After ebony went out of favour for longcase clocks walnut was used, as were laburnum and olivewood which were often cut across the branch in what is known as oyster-cut veneers for use in parquetry. (The term parquetry covers the use of veneers in any geometric design.) The difficulty in cutting large sheets of veneers probably accounts for the large output of inlaid pieces. The finest of the early inlay work was executed by Dutch and French craftsmen working in London. The latter were Huguenot refugees, who had fled from the Continent on the Revocation of the Edict of Nantes (1685).

Plate 48a – A fine 8-day clock by Daniel Quare of London, dating c. 1690. The designs are nicely drawn and many coloured woods are used which produces a lively and realistic appearance. Green stained bone is often used for leaves.

The Eighteenth Century
By the beginning of the eighteenth century numerous types of marquetry had appeared. To save time, two, three or four sheets of veneer would be cut together, so that the waste of one panel formed the ground of the next and vice versa.

England's links with Holland were further strengthened when William of Orange became King of England through his marriage to Mary, the granddaughter of Charles I. During their reign many products of both countries were almost indistinguishable. By the late seventeenth century the Dutch had perfected a method of imitating Chinese lacquer for the decoration of furniture. The technique appears in England by about 1670 but it was not until around 1700 that it was used extensively on clock cases. Deal was used almost exclusively for seventeenth-century lacquered pieces, since the gesso ground adhered to it well. Unfortunately the use of this soft wood has led to a high mortality rate through rot and woodworm. Consequentely, lacquered cases before 1700 are rare. Many blacked pine cases found today were probably originally lacquered. During the eighteenth century oak was increasingly used in the carcasses of lacquered cases.

Plate 48b – A particularly fine example of a rare pale blue lacquered longcase clock c. 1725, by Marwick of London. The elegance and splendour of fine town and country houses is well reflected in this imposing clock which stands over 2·4 m (8 ft) tall. Few clocks of this period have survived with their original elaborate tops and double plinth to the base. Mirror glass was sometimes inset into the trunk door of lacquered longcase clocks at this time. In the past, dealers and collectors alike have believed that many of these lacquered cases were decorated in the East Indies. However, there is no proof of this and it is known that 'japanners' were working in London in the late seventeenth century. In 1694 a contemporary writer notes that 'the Japan is brought to that perfection that it not only outdoes all that is made in India, but also vies for its lacquer with the Japan lacquer itself, and there is hope of imitating its best draught and figures'. Certainly, by the early eighteenth century, there were a great number of japanners to meet the ever-increasing demand. One establishment would build the carcase which would then be sent for decoration to a specialist, such as Richard Jones, at the sign of the 'Japanned Cabinet' near King Edward's Stairs, Wapping, or James Bradford, japanner, at the sign of the 'Angel', Fleet St.

English lacquer tended to be even more colourful than eastern lacquer, because while eastern lacquer was usually dark brown or black, in England the ground colours included black, yellow, dark and pale blue, various reds, olive, dark green, lapis lazuli, imitation tortoiseshell and marble. The quality of a piece depends not only on the fineness of the drawing but also on the smoothness and polish of the ground colour. During the eighteenth century the polishing process was often dispensed with and replaced by varnish which was painted on before the raised and gilt decoration was applied. Consequently many of the later cases are dull in colour because the varnish has turned brown. By 1750 a wide variety of decorative types had been introduced. The *chinoiserie* was not always in relief. Sometimes it was combined with a coloured etching or a painting on canvas to form a centre panel on the trunk door. The whole of the front of a case is sometimes decorated with a polychromatic design of flowers or fruit or with a romantic subject derived from the French rococo artists, Lancret and Watteau.

Plate 49 – A longcase clock movement with its arched dial removed to show the rack striking mechanism, which became universal for 8-day clocks from about 1730. This 8-day movement by Thomas Windmills of London dates from about 1720. A notable point is the sturdy bracket in which the rack itself is pivoted. The tail of the rack is sprung to avoid it being damaged if the clock should be turned past 12 o'clock without striking. The aptly named snail is clearly visible.

Plate 50 – Another clock from the Windmills workshop in Tower Street, London. It was made by Joseph Windmills, the father of Thomas and was intended for the German market where mirror veneered pieces were popular.

During the eighteenth century France was the unrivalled leader of fashion in furniture, interior design and costume. French themes influenced every area of design. That very English cabinet-maker, Thomas Chippendale, and his contemporaries Ince and Mayhew and Vile and Cobb were all much influenced by the French rococo. Unlike many designers who produced pattern books, Chippendale included a number of designs for longcase clocks and bracket clocks. Some of these designs were made and contain movements by some of the leading makers of the day.

Plate 51 – A bracket clock by Archambo and Marchant, London, *c.* 1750. This partnership made both longcase and bracket clocks in cases of carved mahogany taken straight from Chippendale's *Directar*. Although many clocks, especially longcase clocks of provincial manufacture, are loosely described as Chippendale, there are very few which adhere closely to his designs. Chippendale also advocated the tapered trunk for longcase clocks to imitate the French pedestal clock, but examples are exceedingly rare.

Plate 52 – The cartel clock, a true French type, was copied closely in England. This one, *c.* 1760, is a well carved gilt wood model of English make. The workmanship of the case is very close to that of contemporary picture and mirror frames.

Plate 53 – This piece from the Chelsea factory is not a true clock since it contains a watch movement. The Chelsea factory followed French taste very closely, which is not surprising considering that two successive managers, Gouyn and Sprimont, were French.

An influential figure in the second half of the century was Sir William Chambers, who became the greatest official architect of his time. He studied in France under J. F. Blondel in 1749 and then in Italy until 1755. The following year he became the Prince of Wales' tutor and by 1760 he was the King's Architect with Robert Adam. His work always kept rigidly to the strict neoclassicism of his French contemporaries with whom he had worked in Paris. However, he also studied eastern architecture of which he gained first-hand knowledge when, as a young-man, he served with the Swedish East India Co. A survival of his work in this field is the Great Pagoda in the Royal Botanical Gardens at Kew.

Plate 54 – Chambers also designed furniture and clockcases, of which this is a typical example. The first clock of this design was made for the King and is part of a *garniture du chemine* now in Windsor Castle. Chambers' original drawings for this clock show it supported by a pair of winged sphinx. The case was made by Matthew Boulton who, in 1762, built an extensive factory at Soho, near Birmingham, which produced all manner of silver, ormolu and Derbyshire 'Blue John' articles. For his designs he took ideas from the work of men such as Chambers, Flaxman and James Stuart. Both Whitehurst of Derby and the royal clockmaker, Thomas Wright, made movements for Boulton's cases. The pedestal supporting the central urn of this clock is of Derbyshire felspar.

Equally elaborate ormolu clocks were made especially for the Chinese market. The name of James Cox immediately springs to mind in this respect. His ormolu and ormolu-mounted bracket clocks are of superb quality. The designs, however, are often far from classical, and are sometimes extraordinarily imaginative and not always aesthetically successful. The Chinese had a passion for these elaborate clocks and automata, and the Emperor's collection of clocks and mechanical curiosities was outstanding. In the 1930s, during the Sino–Japanese war, Simon Harcourt-Smith was given the enviable task of cataloguing the collection. At that time he was able to report that 'the passage of the hours was marked by the fluttering of enamelled wings, and a gushing of glass fountains, and a spinning of paste stars while from a thousand concealed and whirring orchestras the

Gavottes and Minuets of London society rose strangely into the Chinese air'.

Plate 55 – An ebonised bracket clock by Recordon and Dupont, *c.* 1795. Recordon was Breguet's agent in England, and Recordon and Dupont took over Josia Emery's business in 1795. The painted dial bears Turkish numerals and has a strike/silent lever and a pendulum regulation dial in the arch. The painted dial was known in the late eighteenth century as a 'japanned' dial, as opposed to an enamelled one. The elaborate dome top and the generous use of cast brass mounts is characteristic of clocks made for the Near East. The arched shape to the base, however, is quite unique.

Tortoiseshell veneered cases were among the most elaborate and successful, profusely mounted with gilt metal and surmouted by a hemispherical dome and flambeau finials.

Lantern clocks were also exported to Turkey throughout the eighteenth century. They were fitted with arched dials, and a raised chapter ring and spandrels, as on a longcase clock. The side frets and doors were often decorated with engraved crescent moons.

Plate 56 – The bell top bracket clock was the standard form throughout the century, subject to the expected changes of detail. This ebonised example of *c.* 1780 has a rare Bilston enamelled dial. The enamel is fired onto a moulded copper sheet, and to prevent the surface cracking the dial is screwed to a heavy brass false dial plate. The back plate of the movement is elaborately engraved.

By the late eighteenth century, clocks were not intended to be carried from room to room. The bracket clock would have a set position in the room and no doubt there would be a clock in nearly every room. Consequently the rear of the clock would never be seen and so there was little point in covering the back plate with beautiful and expensive engraving.

Plate 58a – The fusée movement from a bracket clock by J. H. Tyrer, London, *c.* 1830. It is interesting to compare this with the bracket clock movement by James Blackborow of a century before. The early movement strives to keep the back plate quite uncluttered by parts of the mechanism so that we can see the engraving at its best. The late movement has its back plate mounted with heavy securing brackets, a bridge and spring for the striking hammer, a spring for the strike/silent mechanism and a massive pendulum-securing bracket. The only engraving is the maker's signature in the centre of the plate.

Provincial Clockmaking
So far we have covered the more unusual clocks of the eighteenth century, made by makers of repute working in London. By 1700 a number of provincial towns had become quite important regional centres of clockmaking. The leading makers in these towns were usually those who had served their apprenticeship in London and their work is very close to that of London, both in quality and style. It is quite natural that these makers would want to keep in step with changing London fashions and it was no doubt a good selling point if they could advertise their clocks as being in the latest London style. Gradually, as the eighteenth century progressed, provincial centres no longer followed London styles but produced clocks of a distinct character. It is possible with a little study to distinguish, for example, between a longcase made in Bristol and one made in Liverpool or between cases from Wigan and Halifax. The same cannot be said of provincial bracket clocks which, being much less common, tend to follow the London styles much more closely.

Plate 58b – It must not be assumed that clocks made in provincial towns were inferior to London-made clocks. This clock from the Whitehurst workshop is in the style associated with his name. It has a circular, engraved and silvered dial. The mahogany case of fine proportions has an imposing swan neck top and finely carved mouldings, a feature which could possibly be traced back to Chippendale's designs.

Other important centres of clockmaking include Newcastle-upon-Tyne, Liverpool, Manchester, Wigan, Halifax, York and Bristol. Scotland also produced some fine makers. The balloon top longcase clock is a type associated with Edinburgh and Glasgow in the early nineteenth century, where the hood follows the circular form of the dial.

Plate 58b – A fine example of a Scottish longcase clock, this is unusual in that the trunk is built in the form of a fluted Greek Doric column. The maker, James Muirhead of 90 Buchanan Street, Glasgow, was watchmaker to the Queen.

With the popularity of the circular dial it is not surprising that oval dials were introduced in order to accommodate moon phases. To know the phase of the moon was of some importance when travelling at night, and few cared to journey through the countryside when there was no moon. The dial could also be used to show the state of the tide, since the tides are dependent on the moon.

Plate 59a – This clock has a universal tidal dial on which one of the movable pointers is adjusted to the date of the lunar month, while the other is made to point at the appropriate hour on the thin band of numerals seen on the moon disk itself. Once these hands have been adjusted for the port in question the hour of high tide can be read off. This clock of about 1800 has a painted iron dial and is signed Jas. Gowland of Blyth, a coal mining and exporting town on the Northumberland coast. The style of the case could be loosely described as Sheraton.

The Regency

During the early nineteenth century many so-called clockmakers were becoming simply repairers and retailers. At the most they finished and assembled parts produced by factories, and the local cabinet-maker or specialised case maker supplied him with the case.

The painted dials of many of the clocks were fitted to cast iron false plates and were made by Birmingham factories. It is quite likely that some clockmakers ordered their dials from these factories but it is also possible that others would order complete movements or even finished clocks from them. In this case the firms would buy in the movements from other makers in or around Birmingham. The painted decoration on these dials sometimes exhibits very competent brushwork. Some examples are signed and dated on the reverse by the artist.

The simple forms of Regency clocks with their sparsely applied ornament lent themselves admirably to large-scale production, for which cases could be made in batches and then sold to the firms making the movements. Consequently identical cases house movements by many makers.

Plate 61a – One of the most popular low-priced clocks was the spring-driven fusée dial clock. This example, *c* 1800, has a flat wooden dial, painted and signed Alcock and Wright. However the movement was supplied to them by the well-known manufacturers to the trade, Handley and Moore. John Thwaites (later to become Thwaites and Reed) and Robson also supplied fine movements of every kind to London and provincial clockmakers. They also supplied completed clocks together with cases.

Plate 59b – An example of an attempt to produce a cheaper 8-day clock. The good-quality striking movement is enclosed in zinc dust covers. The dial is 20 cm (8 in) wide and signed Taylor and Son. The clock hangs on the wall. The lack of a wooden case kept the price down but also made it a less imposing piece of furniture, which may account for the scarcity of these clocks. Whitehurst and Son of Derby are known to have made some very similar clocks often with circular painted dials.

Plate 61b – A 'drop dial' clock complete with carved 'ears' beneath the dial, which is of painted iron. Regency examples often have delicate brass and ebony, or mother-of-pearl inlay round the dial or on the trunk. This clock by Barwise is of about 1830.

Large weight-driven wall clocks with the pendulum and weights enclosed within the trunk had been made from the early eighteenth century when they were normally lacquered. Such clocks were probably made for assembly rooms, entrance halls of public buildings or any large room where nothing too splendid was required. The dials are very legible, being black with gilt numerals and brass hands, or white with black numerals. Nineteenth-century clocks of this type were encased in mahogany or rosewood and the dial was usually protected by a glass in a brass or wooden bezel.

In London, in the nineteenth century, there was a general decline in the output of longcase clocks. Of those which have survived a considerable number are regulators or striking clocks with regulator escapements. Some of these precision clocks were made for clock and watch repairers and retailers so they could check the clocks in their charge, consequently the cases are very plain and severe in design. There was also a demand for a precision clock for domestic use.

Plate 60a – A fine example of a domestic regulator of the 1830s in an elaborate mahogany and ebony moulded gothic style case ordered, no doubt, to fit in with the gothic decoration of the owner's house. The movement is not of special quality but is massively built. It has a Graham dead beat escapement, maintaining power and a wooden rod pendulum.

Plate 60b – Another domestic clock, again with a dead beat escapement. This clock, however, also strikes the hours and half-hours on a bell. The case is very much in the eighteenth-century style, although the full arch dial is typical of Regency clocks, especially bracket clocks. The zinc dial is painted with roses and forget-me-nots. Both the dial and back plate are signed French, Royal Exchange, London, and the clock dates to *c.* 1820.

If an English clock strikes the half-hour it is usually by a single stroke on the bell. This is most confusing, as a clock will strike one three times in succession between half-past twelve and half-past one.

Benjamin Lewis Vulliamy was one of the leading clockmakers in the early nineteenth century. Like his father and grandfather before him he was clockmaker to the monarch until his death in 1854. He appears to have worked through a great range of cases of French designs, from neoclassical themes in porcelain and marble back to the Louis XIV style, richly ornamented in tortoiseshell marquetry in the manner of Boulle, and mounted in ormolu. He also used the more conventional Regency cases.

Another influential figure was Thomas Hope. His *Household Furniture and Interior Decoration* was the most important design book of the period in England. Unlike its predecessors it was not a pattern-book but an illustrated description of his London home in Portland Place. The rooms were decorated in the Antiquarian Grecian, Roman and Egyptian styles as well as the exotic Chinese and Turkish. His designs were strongly influenced by those of the French Directoire and Empire periods. Hope made no secret of his source of inspiration and referred to his friendship with Charles Percier and Pierre Fontaine, the masters of the Empire style in France. Two design books quickly followed Hope's publication, George Smith's in 1808 and Richard Brown's in 1820.

Plate 62 – This clock, *c.* 1810, is very close in feeling to the designs of Thomas Hope. It includes such architectural features as the classical pediment and Grecian akroter surmounting tapering pedestals. The carving and brass inlay is crisp and néat. The enamelled dial is signed on the reverse by the enameller, Richard Symes. The movement fits tightly into the circular top and is by Desbois and Wheeler of Gray's Inn Passage, London.

Plate 63 – A chamfer top bracket clock by D & W Morice of Cornhill, London, displaying a particularly refined and severe treatment of a classic Regency form. The enamelled dials of Regency clocks are perhaps the most legible of all clock dials.

Plate 64 – This clock made by Viner and Company of London *c.* 1830 is an example of the Gothic revival, a theme which appears as early as Chippendale's *Director*. The Gothic of the eighteenth century is a rustic gothic, in contrast to the hard, uncompromising interpretation of the style this clock displays. Standing about 56 cm (22 in) high it has enamelled dials with Breguet-style hands and a gilt engine-turned surround. The quarter-chiming movement is of massive proportions with a back plate plain except for the maker's name. Cases of identical design to this were made in various sizes, the smallest being little larger than a carriage clock.

Plate 65 – This modest-looking clock is a rare example of a mantel regulator. It has a dead beat escapement, with a large seconds dial, maintaining power and a wooden rod pendulum. The small keyhole within the figure XII is for regulating the pendulum. The silvered brass dial is signed James Tupman, London.

The Victorian Era

The mid-nineteenth century saw dramatic changes in the clock- and watch-making industries in America, Germany and Switzerland. Mechanisation was the only way to provide low-priced articles which everyone could afford. Clocks such as those of the Tupmans and others could only be afforded by the wealthy and professional and business men. The English trade never interested itself in producing decorative clocks for farmworkers or mill and factory workers.

In 1843 the British watch company was founded under the chairmanship of John Barwise. It was the brainchild of the Swiss P. F. Ingold and was to make watches by machine tools. Unfortunately the opposition of Clerkenwell and Coventry, the centres of the British craft, killed the scheme before it was able to prove itself. Ingold subsequently took his ideas to America where they were soon adopted.

John Bennett of 65, Cheapside, was another man who advocated new methods of production to compete with foreign imports. His ideas were most unpopular and he was widely criticised for selling foreign products in his shop, a practice which nearly all retailers were eventually forced to adopt, including such famous names as Dent, Vulliamy, Barraud and Lund, and Frodsham. In 1883 Sir Edmund Beckett warned, in his book *Clocks, Watches and Bells*, that 'Although labour is dearer in America than here this machinery enables them to undersell English watches as the Swiss also do with cheaper labour and more organisation though with less use of machines; and if our English makers do not bestir themselves they will lose the trade in all but the best watches as they have already lost that of both cheap and ornamental clocks'. The English trade had already been hit very badly by the factory-made imports of America, Germany and France.

In fig. 25 we see an engraving of Benson's much advertised steam factory on Ludgate Hill. This was one of the few such factories of the late nineteenth century. In the background is the steam-engine with its huge flywheel driving lathes, vertical drills and other machinery. This was not like factory production in America, since it was really only a streamlining of the old clockmakers' craft. No new methods had been introduced in England such as rolled and stamped-out brass. The main workshop here was for the production of turret clocks, while upstairs watchmakers are finishing and assembling watches.

One very successful quality ornamental clock made in nineteenth-century England as well as in France was the skeleton clock. As the

BENSON'S CLOCK FACTORY.

25. THE ENGRAVING OF BENSON'S FAMOUS STEAM FACTORY ON LUDGATE HILL IN THE 1890s

name implies this has heavy plates cut into decorative shapes allowing all the wheels to be seen. The movement is mounted on a heavy wooden or marble base and displayed beneath a glass shade. Sometimes the opportunity was taken to show off a complicated escapement, while others were made with nests of bells chiming the quarter-hours, but mostly they were timepieces or simply struck the hour on one bell or a gong.

Plate 66 – This skeleton clock is made in the form of Lichfield Cathedral. It has a dead beat escapement and a mercury pendulum for temperature compensation. The dial is also cut out in a Gothic style to reveal the striking lifting pieces on the front plate. As a result,

"The Elizatethan.

9839b.—Registered Design.

26. LONGCASE CLOCK
MODELLED ON 'BIG BEN'
WHICH RETAILED IN THE
1890S FOR £110

27. THE 'ELIZABETHAN'. A
QUARTER-CHIMING
LONGCASE CLOCK FROM
THE CATALOGUE OF
S. SMITH AND SON, *c*. 1900

it is, like most skeleton clocks, almost impossible to see the position of the hands.

In the late Victorian period there was a revival in the popularity of carved furniture, inspired by Ruskin's ideals. Ruskin, who had considerable influence upon popular taste in art and design, hated machine work and believed that the beauty of Gothic architecture resulted from the pleasure enjoyed by the workmen engaged in its construction. He and Pugin were the leaders of the nineteenth-century Gothic revival. Pugin had been employed by Barry to design all the Gothic detail and fittings for the present Houses of Parliament after the old Palace of Westminster was destroyed by fire in 1834. Perhaps the ultimate in Gothic design cases is that advertised in the 1890s and seen in fig. 26. It is a longcase clock made as a miniature of the great clock tower at Westminster.

Other heavily-carved styles appeared at this time variously known as Elizabethan, Louis XIV, Chippendale and Louis XV, none of which bear any resemblance to the styles which are supposed to have been their inspiration. They are all typically late Victorian, of good quality but of heavy design and badly proportioned. Some of these cases contain fine quality English fusée movements of immense weight, but similar clocks were imported from Germany and contain much lighter German movements without fusées.

7

U.S.A.

Clockmaking in the Pioneering Days

In the past collectors and historians have dismissed American clocks as inferior to the contemporary European products. As such they were not considered worthy of further investigation until recent years when their true importance in American history was understood. Even today few but the Americans themselves who show any appreciation of their products of the latter part of the nineteenth century.

In the seventeenth and eighteenth centuries clocks were modelled closely on European products. This was only natural, for many clockmakers in the early days received their training in Europe before they arrived in America. Many of these pioneering craftsmen not only made clocks but also provided other services related to their skill as metalworkers. Among these would undoubtedly be that of bellfounder and locksmith, as well as the essentials of gunsmithing and blacksmithing.

Domestic clocks in the early eighteenth century were an expensive item, the raw materials probably accounting for a large proportion of the price of the article. As might be expected, the spring-driven clock was made only in very small numbers, for the making of the coiled spring and the fusée posed considerable difficulties then. In fact, springs had to be imported until 1830 when they were first manufactured in America. By the late eighteenth century many tools and some clock parts were imported, but it is unlikely that this would have occurred to any great extent at the beginning of the century.

Between 1700 and 1740 the clock trade grew rapidly and many specialist craftsmen produced tall clocks, which certainly equalled the work of most provincial clockmakers in England. Case and movement design showed little sign of departing from English tradition. Mahogany was the most popular wood for casemaking, though cherry and walnut were occasionally used. Some cases were veneered; others were lacquered and decorated with gilt *chinoiserie* designs.

Plate 67a – A mid-eighteenth century tall clock by Isaac Doolittle who completed his apprenticeship in 1742 and in the same year opened a shop on Chapel Street, New Haven. He died in 1800 aged 79. The case is of solid mahogany with ogee feet and an elaborate swan neck cresting with three finials. The brass dial is very similar to contemporary London-made dials, and is signed on the segment-shaped plaque in the lower half of the dial centre. The brass movement is of 8-day duration and strikes the hours.

A National Style Evolves
From the mid-eighteenth century a truly American style of cabinet-making began to evolve which was also reflected in clock case designs. Although tall clock cases of this period are somewhat similar to those of, say, Liverpool or Birmingham in England, the American cases are unique in a number of respects. The block front, in particular, distinguishes the finer American tall clocks from the products of any other country. As can be seen from the drawing the block front

28. THE BLOCK FRONT

consists of a shallow bowed front to the trunk door which is topped with a carved voluted shell motif. The arched hoods are usually surmounted with a scrolled pediment of more exaggerated proportions than is usual on English clocks. It is uncommon to find brass mounts of any sort on these cases but there is correspondingly greater use of carved ornamentation.

The capabilities of American craftsmen are demonstrated in the work of David Rittenhouse of Philadelphia (1732–96), who was the most celebrated maker of his day. He was chiefly a scientist and astronomer, making scientific instruments as well as clocks. His masterpiece is a magnificent astronomical chiming tall clock housed with the Drexel Institute of Technology, Philadelphia. This clock is of superlative quality and is contained in a beautifully carved Chippendale-style mahogany case.

Plate 67b – A tall clock made by Thomas Harland of Norwich, Connecticut, *c.* 1790. The solid cherry wood case is a magnificent example of the cabinet work associated with the Norwich area. The arch topped hood has a decorative fret work design known as 'whale's tails', and three carved wooden finials. The 8-day brass movement has an engraved silvered brass dial with the moon's phases in the arch.

Thomas Harland settled in America from England in 1773, and opened a shop in Norwich in that year. Baillie's *Watchmakers and Clockmakers of the World* records that he left London for America so he may have been trained in London. Harland is said to have used early forms of mass production methods in his business. One of his numerous apprentices was Daniel Burnap who in his turn took on as an apprentice Eli Terry, the father of American mass-produced clockmaking.

Post-Revolution Federal America
The Revolution somewhat disrupted the clock trade and many clockmakers started making bullets and guns. After the Revolution materials were scarce and therefore expensive. The price of brass towards the end of the century made the tall clock uneconomical, and a few makers eventually turned to wood as an

alternative material for making, not only the clock plates, but also the wheels. The clearest way to illustrate this progress in the trade in the following decades is to trace the career of Eli Terry.

Terry was born in 1772 and apprenticed to Daniel Burnap of East Windsor, Connecticut. In 1793 he started in business on his own at Plymouth. Terry's importance in clockmaking history is due not only to his inventiveness but also to the fact that he was an astute business-man. He invented and perfected the wooden movement. Apart from the change in materials and the proportions of the parts, the con-struction of the movements remained basically unchanged.

Plate 67c – A tall clock by Eli Terry in a solid cherry wood case. The style of the case owes not a little to current London designs, with quarter columns in the trunk corners and a pagoda top to the hood. The case contains a 30-hour pull-wind wood movement. The dial is also of wood with a facing of printed and hand-coloured paper. Terry's name is in the calendar dial. The hands are of cast pewter.

Terry made both brass and wood movements but had discontinued the former by about 1800. He realised that there was a huge potential market for a reasonably priced clock and so he slowly began intro-ducing more streamlined methods of production. In 1800 he was using water-power to drive his saws and other equipment. By 1807, according to Jerome, he was producing 200 clocks a year. This was a revolution in production methods, since each clock was no longer made to order, but it was practicable to make the goods and then afterwards think about promoting sales. Chauncey Jerome, in *History of the U.S. Clock Business*, tells how people ridiculed Terry. 'The foolish man they said had begun to make 200 clocks; one said "he would never live long enough to make them" and another that "he would nor could possibly sell so many".' At first each movement was sold without a case, and the customer had to case it himself. Or it could be hung on the wall, and it was then known as a 'wag on the wall', a term applied to any wall clock the weights and pendulum of which are not encased.

Following Terry's success an increasing number of makers pro-duced wooden clocks in large numbers using primitive machinery. This increased competition and inevitably put many small concerns out of business, for the price of clocks had been more than halved by the new techniques.

In 1814 Terry 'invented' a shelf clock known as the pillar and scroll clock. In American horology new case designs as well as mechanical ones were regarded as inventions. This style of case was very popular in Connecticut between about 1818 to 1830. The weight-driven movements were normally of wood, and the weights are suspended on cords which ran over pulleys at the top of the box-like case in order to gain the maximum drop.

Plate 68 – A pillar and scroll clock make by Ephraim Downes for George Mitchell of Bristol, Connecticut. The wooden weight-driven movement is of thirty hours duration. Downes was a wood movement manufacturer in Bristol and supplied clocks to George Mitchell who was a prominent merchant. According to Kenneth D. Roberts in *Eli Terry and the Connecticut shelf clock*, Downes made 3,002 clocks for Mitchell between March 1826 and February 1828.

Terry was by no means the first to introduce a new design. Simon Willard (1753–1848) of Grafton, Massachusetts, was a maker who continued to use brass for his movements in which he took great pride. He made a 30-hour wall clock which developed into the Massachusetts shelf clock. In order to save brass his wall movements were circular. The design of these weight-driven wall clocks was not unlike a bracket clock standing on a large wall bracket which housed the weight and pendulum. The step from this wall clock to the shelf clock variety was a very small one.

Plate 69a – One of Simon Willard's later banjo clocks, made in Roxbury, Massachusetts, in the 1820s. The case is faced with simple curved section mouldings forming panels filled with delicately painted glass panels. The waist is flanked by long brass scrolls which give the impression that they are supporting the dial.

Plate 69b – A lyre clock made by Samuel Abbot of Montpelier, Vermont, and so inscribed on the dial. This piece is dated 1810 and has an 8-day brass weight-driven movement. The lyre clock is a development from the banjo type. This is a typical example with vigorously carved lyre-shaped scrolls and leaves forming the trunk.

172

In the late 1790s Simon Willard produced a new clock design, known today as the banjo clock. It was not patented until 1802 and was always known as the 'Improved Patent Timepiece'. From about 1802 Simon Willard abandoned the production of other clocks to concentrate on the banjo clock which was immediately successful. He is believed to have made some four thousand of these clocks. The brass movements were well-made, and almost invariably they were timepieces only and did not strike. Some alarm clocks were also made.

The banjo and lyre clocks are without doubt two of the most beautiful of American clocks. The finest development of the banjo clock was the girandole, where the lower part of the clock was circular rather than rectangular and supported on a carved and gilded bracket of acanthus leaves. The whole design had an extra touch of grace and quality. The glass panels were often painted with scenes from classical mythology and there was an increased use of gilt for the mouldings. However the trend during the early nineteenth century was towards simplicity and economy. This can be seen especially in the decline of style and beauty of the later lyre clocks.

Plate 70a – A Massachusetts shelf clock by Aaron Willard of Boston made *c.* 1800. The mahogany case is finely veneered and the upper section follows the outline of the kidney-shaped dial. The brass weight-driven movement is of 8-day duration.

The Massachusetts shelf clock was made between the late 1780s to about 1830 and vary stylistically considerably over this period. Eighteenth-century examples are often made to look like belltop or archtop bracket clocks on a large base or stand. Later examples unite the two parts and the base often contains a painted glass panel to match the decoration around the dial.

American makers were now seeking cheapness of production but there were also some inventive and scientific minds at work, notably Joseph Ives. It was he who had 'invented', or introduced to American clockmaking, roller pinions for wooden movements. His most important contribution was the introduction of rolled brass which was to be a great step forward in production methods. Before this was introduced he had experimented with iron-plated movements using cast brass wheels and later still, in 1859, with tin-plate movements. The coiled spring was not used in mass-produced American clocks till about 1850, but about 1825 Ives introduced his wagon spring clock.

Plate 70b – An early wagon spring clock by Joseph Ives, made between 1823 and 1830 at Brooklyn, Long Island, New York. It has the early style movement with cut and filed wrought sheet brass plates. Later movements had plates of riveted strips of brass, the so-called 'ladder' type movement. The movement has roller pinions as invented by Ives and the wagon spring is mounted in the bottom section of the case.

Another invention which this time led the world was Aaron Crane's torsion clock. Instead of using a swinging pendulum to control the rate of the clock, he devised a balance suspended from the movement by a wire which twisted first one way and then the other. This principle was later used very successfully by the Germans. Crane's clocks were made with eight-day or one month's duration and sometimes, as with German torsion clocks, a year, and were also an early example of the use of a coiled spring for their going power. These clocks utilised a fusée.

Plate 71 – The principle of the wagon spring clock was used as early as 1680 in France, but it is most unlikely that Joseph Ives was aware of its earlier application. Its action is quite simple. A laminated spring, similar to a wagon spring, is securely bolted to the bottom of the case. The ends are attached indirectly through a lever system to the barrels of the two trains of wheels so that on winding the clock, the ends of the spring are pulled up under tension. The lever system serves to amplify the movement of the spring. This clock was made by Birge and Fuller of Bristol, *c*. 1845. It is just over two foot high.

Dr Benjamin Franklin, the well-known American philosopher, was also responsible for a particular clock design. He was born in Boston, Massachusetts, in 1706 and visited London several times after 1750. When in London he became a close friend of James Ferguson who designed many astronomical and tidal clocks. It is thought that the horological work of Ferguson inspired Franklin to design a clock which could be simply and economically constructed.

174

Plate 72 a and b – A clock made in America to Dr Franklin's design. There are only three wheels in the train: a great wheel which carries the winding pulley, an intermediate wheel of 120 teeth and an escape wheel of 30 teeth which, with its seconds pendulum, shows true seconds on the dial in the arch. To the great wheel arbor is fixed the single hand from which both hours and minutes can be easily read. This hand goes round once every 4 hours. The design of this clock dispenses with motion work behind the dial. The plates of the movement are of wrought iron and the clock is hung on the wall and has no case. The movement is protected from dirt and dust by a tin cover fixed to the back of the painted cast iron dial.

Mass-produced Brass Clocks

In 1837 the great monetary panic and subsequent depression for a short time brought clockmaking to a standstill, and indeed many wondered if the business would ever recover. During this time Chauncey Jerome of Bristol, Connecticut, who had earlier worked for Terry, designed the 30-hour O.G. shelf clock.

This clock had a rolled brass 30-hour weight-driven movement, and can be considered to be a descendant of the pillar and scroll clock. Its simplicity and cheapness revived the industry and was soon copied by many factories. The way the clocks were made in the Jerome factory is interesting. All the pine for the case was cut into the required width on a circular saw, the lengths were then run over the planing machine and then through the O.G. cutter, which formed the shape of the front of the case. The veneer was glued onto these lengths which were clamped together, one shape fitting into another, for the glue to set. The O.G. shape was then sanded on shaped wheels onto which sandpaper had been pasted. The lengths were then ready for varnishing and mitreing to the correct size. At the height of production Jerome had the materials for 10,000 of these cases in the works at any one time. The case cost 50 cents. The dials were punched out of thin sheets of zinc and the numerals printed on and twelve to fifteen hundred could be printed in a day. The designs on the glass doors were also printed and then coloured by hand. The complete clock cost about two dollars. Jerome believed that he had the most advanced factories in America for clock production.

Plate 72c – A 30-hour O.G. clock in a mahogany veneered case produced by the Waterbury Clock Co. of Waterbury, Connecticut. The painted zinc dial is decorated with a printed blue design in the spandrels. Quite often the graining was faked onto US clocks and varnished. Slightly larger O.G. cases were made to house 8-day movements.

Plate 72d – A rosewood veneered 8-day column shelf clock by Seth Thomas who had a factory at Plymouth Hollow. Thomas was one of Jerome's big competitors and Plymouth Hollow was renamed Thomaston in his honour in 1865. This clock was made after this since it contains a label giving his address as Thomaston. Both the 30-hour O.G. and the column clocks were suitable as either wall or shelf clocks. This example stands 32 inches high (81 cms).

The coiled spring allowed clocks to be made very much smaller and opened the door to a rush of new designs. At the same time, the American exhibits at the Great Exhibition at Crystal Palace in 1851 boosted demand. Elias Ingraham was an important designer of cases and it was he who introduced the Gothic 'Steeple' clock shown in plate 71.

Plate 73a – Ingraham's original steeple clock design had free-standing pillars at the corners of the case. The clock illustrated here, by Jerome of New Haven, is a simplified version veneered in mahogany. It strikes the hours and has an alarm mechanism. The alarm setting disk is in the centre of the dial while the alarm mechanism is a separate movement screwed to the back of the case, below the clock movement proper.

It is interesting to compare this steeple clock design and other designs with contemporary or earlier English bracket clock designs. The steeple clock can be compared with the Gothic style clock in plate 64, the English lancet top became the American beehive or Tudor clock, the arch top became the American rounded top and the four glass bracket clock design evolved into the cheapest of American shelf clocks seen in plate 73b.

Plate 73b – This clock must have been one of the lowest priced models of all. It stands nine inches high and has a brass 30-hour movement. Notice the novel idea of incorporating the maker's initials in the design of the hands. The maker is, of course, Seth Thomas.

It was not only English designs which inspired the designers of American clocks. Almost every popular type of European clock was eventually copied in an attempt to capture an even wider market. Cheap imitations of the Vienna wall regulator were so popular in Holland that they helped kill the Dutch clockmaking industry in the late nineteenth century.

The catalogue plates shows two of the 500 models made by the Ansonia Clock Co. by 1914. Their catalogue for that year is a

29. THE 'ENVOY'. A FOUR-GLASS MANTEL CLOCK FROM THE ANSONIA CLOCK COMPANY CATALOGUE OF 1914

30. DIANA BALL SWING. A
MYSTERY SWINGING BALL
CLOCK FROM THE ANSONIA
CLOCK COMPANY
CATALOGUE OF 1914

book of some 140 pages from which a customer could choose a clock costing from 2 dollars to 300 dollars.

Plate 73c – The very popular French marble clock was copied in America although marble was rarely used in its construction. The American factories imitated marble with enamelled iron or, as here, with painted wood. It must be remembered that the movements were of stamped-out rolled brass and bear little resemblance to the fine quality French ones.

Plate 73d – A few makers introduced the fusée into one or two of their models. This illustration shows a fusée movement in a steeple clock as advertised by Jerome around 1850. The movement is the standard one with added brackets to take the spring barrels. The fusée itself takes the place of the normal open coiled spring on the great wheel arbor. The gut line is clearly visible. The fusées are very badly shaped, with hardly any variation in their diameter from one end to the other. It seems likely that American makers thought that a fusée clock would sell better in England where the fusée was so highly regarded.

During the last thirty years of the nineteenth century American factories produced a range of imaginative novelty clocks. Some of the most sought after today are the blinking eye clocks. They consist of painted cast iron figures where the clock dial forms the body of a musical instrument. A well known pair is Topsey and Sambo. Topsey, a dancer, holds in her hand a tambourine, while Sambo plays the banjo.

Fig. 31 shows an old photograph taken in the early 1900s of a country clock and watch repairer's shop. There must have been many such small businesses throughout Europe which specialised in selling the cheaper clocks of America and the Black Forest area of Germany. Here we see Mr Lloyd in front of his shop in the high street of Llanfyllin in Montgomery, Wales. In the window are displayed a range of spring-driven shelf clocks. On the back of the bottom shelf is a marble French clock and a Black Forest cuckoo clock.

Plate 74a – A clock made by the Ansonia Clock Co. in imitation of the French style. Notice especially the visible Brocot-type escapement and the paper dial which gives the impression of enamel very convincingly. The 'marble' base is enamelled iron, while the 'ormolu' figure and mounts are finished with what the catalogue describes as a Japanese Bronze Finish.

Plate 74b – An example of the late nineteenth-century drop dial wall clock in a walnut case with satinwood inlaid lines. Wall clock cases of this sort were marketed in England where they were very popular. Compared with the cases of English fusée wall clocks it is

31. COUNTRY CLOCK SHOP OF THE EARLY 1900S SELLING THE CHEAPER AMERICAN BLACK FOREST PRODUCTS

flimsy and poorly finished. The movement of this clock is by the New Haven Clock Co., and the name, W. Harris of Knighton, on the dial is that of the retailer who had a shop in Broad Street in 1887.

Plate 74c – An American clock of unusually fine quality. The heavy solid brass case is inspired by French four glass clocks. The dial is enamelled and the movement, which is circular in shape, is signed by the Ansonia Clock Co., New York. The springs are encased within brass drums and are mounted between separate plates, so that the springs can be replaced without dismantling the whole movement.

The pin pallet watch-like escapement is also mounted separately on the back plate. The clock strikes the hours on a coiled gong.

The list of clocks seems as endless as the materials with which the cases were made. Bracket or mantle and wall clock cases were often made of papier mâché inset with mother-of-pearl and painted with flowers. Nineteenth-century American clocks were of lesser quality than English clocks of that period, and although handsome when new, time did not treat them kindly. They were, however, serviceable and their low cost made them available to many who could not afford clocks of higher quality.

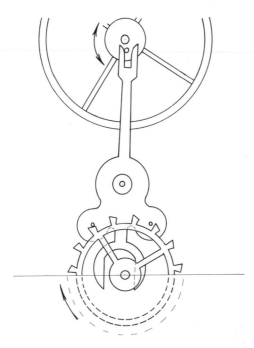

32. A PIN PALLET ESCAPEMENT USED ON SOME CHEAP NINETEENTH-CENTURY AMERICAN CLOCKS

8

Japan

The Japanese Calendar and System of Time Measurement

To understand antique Japanese clocks it is necessary to have a knowledge of the Japanese system of time reckoning. In Europe the period of the day and night is divided into twenty-four equal hours. Until 1873 the Japanese divided this same period into twelve 'hours'. Daylight was divided into six hours and so was the period of darkness. Thus, in midsummer, the daylight hours were very much longer than the hours of darkness. Japanese clocks were devised using several methods to allow for the changing length of the hours. It is interesting to note that the period of daylight was considered to include both the dawn and twilight. Using the stars as a gauge, dawn commenced when the stars were no longer visible and similarly twilight ended as the stars appeared. The hours were known as 'toki' which was divided into ten 'buns' which in turn, for greater accuracy were divided into ten 'rin'.

The twelve hours were numbered nine-four twice over in descending order with the number nine, with its supposedly magical properties, denoting the fixed moments of midday and midnight. Associated with each hour of the day and night was, as well as the numeral, one of the twelve Chinese signs of the zodiac. Many clock dials display both the numerals and the zodiac signs. The half hours were often sounded by the clock with one stroke on the bell after the uneven numbered hours and with two strokes after the evenly numbered ones.

182

The following chart shows the information given by most Japanese clocks. The hours and zodiac signs are, of course, denoted by Japanese characters and not by the Arabic numerals given here.

hrs.	½ hrs.	zodiac		hrs.	½ hrs.	zodiac	
6		Hare	Dawn	6		Cock	Dusk
	2				2		
5		Dragon		5		Dog	
	1				1		
4		Serpent		4		Boar	
	2				2		
9		Horse	Midday	9		Rat	Midnight
	1				1		
8		Goat		8		Bull	
	2				2		
7		Ape		7		Tiger	
	1				1		

The Introduction of the Mechanical Clock

Mechanical clocks appear to have been introduced into Japan by European traders. It was not until 1542 that the Portuguese discovered Japan and, like all the European seafaring nations, their chief aim was to develop trade. The Portuguese were followed by the Spanish and later by the Dutch who opened a trading station in Japan in 1605. In 1613 the English East India Company followed suit, but the Dutch competition was too great and the company abandoned the venture after some ten years.

Among the first clocks to reach Japan would have been those brought as gifts by the Jesuit missionaries who, because of their close connections with Rome, would no doubt have had Italian clocks. Spain and Portugal were not clockmaking centres and from examination of early Japanese clocks it appears that they used Dutch models. Certainly they are very closely based on European weight-driven clocks. At first, no doubt, the Japanese regarded European clocks as curiosities and little more than elaborate toys since the European system of hours and minutes bore no relation to their own method of measuring time. Among the missionaries who arrived in Japan there may well have been trained clockmakers who could pass on their skills to the local craftsmen, for as well as spreading the Gospel, the Jesuits always contributed other skills to the community among which they worked. The Japanese were particularly skilled metal-workers and even without outside guidance, combined with the extraordinary ease with which they were, and still are, able to reproduce foreign articles, the production of a clock would not have posed too great a problem.

However, very few people in Japan needed timepieces since society was ordered very much as it had been in medieval Europe. Clocks were always a luxury item enjoyed only by the very wealthy. Indeed they are so scarce in Japan today that many Japanese do not know of the existence of antique clocks in their country. The scarcity of examples makes their study and dating very difficult, although some landmarks in their development can be found.

The Japanese Lantern Clock

The so-called Japanese lantern clocks appear to have been the first clocks to be made in Japan and were very close in construction to Dutch weight-driven chamber clocks. Small examples could be hung on the wall but it was more usual for them to be placed on a stand on the floor. Since it was customary to sit on the floor the stands are no more than 18–24 in (45–60 cm) in height. It is quite possible that the enclosed pyramidal stands are the earliest style made of decorated lacquered wood. Later stands supported the clock on four legs and were made of lacquered wood, with the legs sometimes carved into the form of trees. Occasionally the stands were of blue and white porcelain, but few of these have survived. As well as having the movement enclosed by tightly fitting doors at the sides the movement is usually given added protection from dust by a glazed hood which matches the stand decoratively. The short drop which the weight is allowed means that many of these lantern clocks require winding as much as twice a day.

Plate 75a – Japanese print depicting a courtier attending an old man seated on the floor reading. Behind the figures stands a lantern clock, with a single foliot balance, supported on a wooden stand. This clock does not have matching glazed hood to protect it.

Plate 75b – Another contemporary Japanese record of a lantern clock, a painting on a silk scroll by Nishikawa Sukenobu (1671–1751). The clock which the lady is winding has a single foliot balance and a fixed dial with a single hand.

Lantern clocks were made as early as the seventeenth century when they were made of iron. It is extremely rare to find any Japanese clock signed by its maker. Eighteenth-century movements are normally of brass and their cases may also be of brass, often beautifully engraved with chrysanthemums in the asymmetric compositions which the western world has come to admire so much. The clock on a stand would be placed fairly centrally within the room where all its sides could be seen. Some cases are of plain silvered copper.

Lantern clocks were almost invariably controlled by a foliot even into the nineteenth century. Some have two foliot balances, one for use during the day and the other at night, the striking mechanism effects the changeover from the one to the other. Such clocks have a fixed dial and hour numerals with a single hand which makes one revolution a day. The weights on the foliots have to be adjusted every two weeks as the length of the day and night alters.

Plate 75c – A lantern clock on a stand not unlike that seen in the print in plate 75a. The matching hood of hardwood, oak or sycamore, is beautifully made and finished. The side and rear windows are fitted with delicate brass fretwork of flowers. This clock also has its original weights of unusual and decorative form. The movement is controlled by a double foliot and has a dial which rotates past a fixed pointer. The 4-poster movement of brass is fitted with four extra decorative turned pillars at the corners. An unusual feature of this clock is its striking action. The last two strokes of the hour are sounded in quick succession to indicate that it has stopped striking. This is achieved by an extra hammer lifted by pins on the count-wheel. This sytem of striking imitates the way in which the hours were sounded in the temples by hand.

If a clock had a single foliot it would require a dial with adjustable numerals as seen in plate 76. Between the hour numerals are half-hour divisions, all of which are a friction tight fit. Each plate has an extension which protrudes behind the dial, and serves as a lifting pin to release the striking mechanism.

The foliot on a lantern clock is a most important part of its visual appearance and it may be for this reason that the less imposing balance wheel or pendulum was not used. It is believed that decorative turning in metal was not practised in Japan until the 1830s. If this is correct all the clocks with fancy turned corner pillars can be assumed to be later. This includes some lantern clocks and the great majority of spring-driven table clocks and pillar wall clocks.

Spring-driven Bracket Clocks

The construction of the bracket or 'pillow' clock is based on that of the lantern clock, except that it is spring-driven and it is wider than it is tall. This means that the fusée is placed beside the spring barrel and not above it as in comparable European clocks. The balance wheel is the most common regulator employed in bracket clocks.

Plate 76 a and b – Two views of the same clock. The upper picture shows the clock in its perfectly fitting wooden case, about 6 inches high. Both the front and the rear panels of the case run in grooves in the sides and can slide out. The finish of the woodwork and the metal work of Japanese clocks is usually of the highest standard and this clock is no exception. The front and back plates are finely engraved. The dial has only hour numerals and consequently only strikes the hours. The numerals are, of course, adjustable. The balance wheel which is encased within the shallow drum, mounted on the top plate has provision for regulation.

The lower picture shows the clock out of its case and seen from the rear. The back plate is engraved similarly to the front one. The notched count-wheel for the striking can be seen. The going train fusée set up ratchet can be seen to the left, while the going barrel ratchet for the striking train is to the right-hand side.

Plate 77 – This interesting clock does not have a balance, but uses a short bob pendulum with a verge escapement. It, too, has a wooden case very like the preceding example, and the back plate is also engraved in a similar manner. Only the going train uses a fusée. The front plate of this clock is very beautifully decorated with cloisonné enamel which was a technique introduced into Japan in the late 1830s. The shallow angular bell is also a nineteenth-century feature. Earlier bells are deeper and almost hemispherical in shape. The drawer in the base contains the winding key. The apertures above the dial are for the calendar. The pierced brass 'fence' around the base of this clock is quite unusual and very effective. The use of fretted brass was a favourite method of decorating clock cases and plates.

Occasionally spring-driven clocks were made with a musical box contained within the base which would be released by the clock mechanism. This idea was probably inspired by European imports as were the few Japanese clocks made to play tunes on a nest of bells.

The Pillar Wall Clock
The pillar clock is the second type of weight-driven clock made in Japan. They are also known as 'foot rule' clocks, many of them being of that length. They can also be found as large as four feet in length. This form of clock may well have been produced as a cheaper form of timepiece for the less well off, many of them being exceedingly plain and simple.

The pillar clock has been likened to a pencil box and a longcase clock. It is simply a long box hung from a nail on the wall, on top of which is mounted an ordinary weight-driven timepiece mechanism of diminutive size. The trunk has a slot cut down its front through which shows a pointer attached to the driving weight. This pointer registers against the hour numerals as it descends. Needless to say, these clocks are of one-day duration although they often have 13-hour numerals so that there is at least an hour in which to re-wind the clock. The key is housed in a small drawer at the base of the trunk.

Plate 78a – This very simple type of pillar clock has the strap form of movement screwed to the back board. This is an early pillar clock, possibly of the eighteenth century. The movement is made wholly of iron and is controlled by a tiny foliot with adjustable weights. The clock is wound by the miniature cranked handle on the front plate.

The hinged wooden hood is here seen opened. The adjustable hour plates can be seen down the front of the wooden trunk, reading from top to bottom 6, 5, 4, 9, 8, 7 twice over.

Plate 78b – A very much more sophisticated and beautiful example of a pillar clock, with the dial in the form of a graduated scale. The table on the trunk has the twelve months across the top. Midwinter is on the left and midsummer on the right, where the night hours are very short, and back from right to left to complete the year. The pointer on the descending bar has to be set by hand to the appropriate month or half month. The hour scale is down the left-hand side of the table with the corresponding zodiac signs to the right. With this form of dial the only adjustments required are the half-monthly ones of the hour pointer.

The balance wheel of this clock is contained within the shallow drum above the movement and fine regulation can be made by means of two small adjustable weights. The balance is fitted with a hair spring. This clock is about 16 inches high. The most striking feature of this clock is the beautifully fretted and engraved front plate, and also the decorative pillars at the corners.

It is quite usual for pillar clocks to have decorative corner pillars or half-pillars but it must be remembered that they are only decorative and do not serve a functional purpose. Since there is no dial on the front plate of the movement this area can be used to display the engraver's skill to great effect. The shape of such engraved and pierced plates bears no relation to its function but is determined by the twists and curls of the leaves and flowers of the design. In this respect the front plate of a pillar clock can be compared with the backcock of an eighteenth-century European watch.

Striking pillar clocks are as ingenious as they are rare. To incorporate a weight-driven striking train in a pillar clock would have required a radical change in its proportions and also a great increase in its weight. These problems were both overcome by constructing a spring-driven striking mechanism within the driving weight of the going train. The striking part enclosed in its brass box was therefore a substitute for the usual lead weight of the clock. At the hour the striking mechanism was released in the same way as on any other clock – by the small inward projections on the reverse of each movable hour plate. Large clocks were also sometimes provided with half-hour plates.

Plate 79 – This small spring-driven clock is constructed within an inrō. The inrō was a small box made in very many shapes and sizes, usually with several compartments which fit tightly together, and was used to carry small items required during the day, serving much the same purpose as a pocket. It was hung from the girdle and was secured by means of the netsuke. An inrō containing a clock such as the one illustrated is therefore the equivalent of the European pocket watch of the period.

The inrō is made of brass and has the remains of polychrome skin or leather covering. The netsuke is of a grotesque face in bronze and silver with an ivory surround. The matching toggle or ojime is signed in silver.

The spring-driven fusée movement fills its case and has a balance-controlled verge escapement. A single figure on the rotating dial, the numerals of which are adjustable, shows through a hole in the case.

The revolution of 1866 opened Japan to western influences in very many areas of life, including the adoption of the western calendar and system of time measurement in 1873. Unless they could be converted, all the clocks we have discussed became obsolete at this time. Most of them were disposed of to dealers in Japanese art and curios, who apparently found a ready market among European and American travellers and collectors. This explains why today these clocks are more common in Europe than they are in Japan. Some of the ones found today will have been converted to the western form of striking the hours from 1–12. The clocks could still be used today for telling the time so long as the numerals were equally spaced and the half-hour numerals were registered as hour divisions.

9 *China*

The ancient civilisation of China has produced many wonderful things which have been the envy of Europe. Porcelain, for instance, was first made in China perhaps around the year AD 800, and yet it was not until the sixteenth century that a reasonably satisfactory copy was produced in Europe. Lacquered decoration on wood has been practised in China since at least the seventh century BC. In the seventeenth century, when the East India Companies began importing it from China, it was immediately copied in Holland and England.

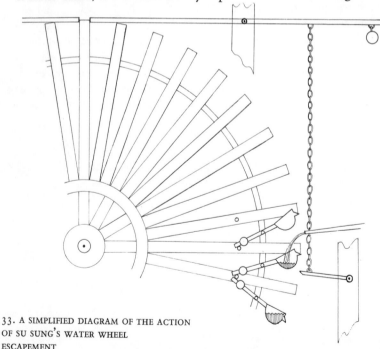

33. A SIMPLIFIED DIAGRAM OF THE ACTION
OF SU SUNG'S WATER WHEEL
ESCAPEMENT

It is seldom realised that a certain Su Sung developed a clock with a form of mechanical-cum-hydraulic escapement as early as around 1090. It used running water to regulate the clockwork of toothed wooden wheels. A later waterwheel had, instead of the usual vanes or troughs, weighted see-saws with buckets on the lighter ends. It was not until the bucket was full of water that it tipped and in doing so released a brake which allowed the whole wheel to turn until the next bucket was in position (see fig. 33). This crude form of escapement could have been of great importance if it had been developed further. Unfortunately it appears that it was an isolated example of one man's ingenuity, the principles of which were lost in the following centuries.

The Introduction of Mechanical Clocks to China

In the sixteenth century, when the first European traders arrived in the country, China's culture had remained virtually unchangd for very many centuries; other cultures were regarded as inferior and contacts with other countries were always tentative and guarded. Foreigners were not allowed freely into the country since China's rulers did not want the way of life disrupted by alien ideas. Permission to enter the country had to be granted by the mandarin of the region in question and was only granted if the foreigner was going to be of special value to the community. China was willing to take what she needed from other nations, but jealously guarded her own assets.

The secret of porcelain production was an example. The export of porcelain in the seventeenth and eighteenth centuries provided a source of great revenue and those who were engaged in its production were formed into monastic-like communities sworn to secrecy and threatened with terrible tortures if caught divulging information. The story goes that one method of punishment was for the culprit to be covered in a mass of porcelain and slowly cooked in a kiln.

The Chinese took a great interest in the mechanical clocks which arrived with the Europeans in the sixteenth century. The Jesuit missionaries used this interest as a way of gaining entry into the country. In 1582 they approached the Viceroy of Kwantung and Kwangsi to inform him that they would like to present him with gifts, among which was a clock which struck the hours. Eventually the missionaries reached the imperial court and presented the Emperor himself with two clocks. The first was a large iron weight-driven chamber clock, the second a small gilt bronze spring-driven table clock. Before very long the Jesuits were instructing four eunuchs of the court in the making of clocks – a superb opportunity of prolonging their stay and gaining a permanent foothold in China.

It must be remembered that the Chinese never considered European clocks as being useful time-measuring instruments, since they had a very different system of hours, somewhat similar to that of the Japanese. Mechanical clocks were considered simply as elaborate toys or curiosities. The term eventually used to describe them was 'self-ringing bell'. Consequently those clocks which contained elaborate chiming musical or automata movements were especially prized.

Having begun trading activities with China the Europeans found difficulty in producing goods to interest the Chinese in exchange for the silks, spices, tea, lacquered objects and porcelain which poured into European ports. It was mainly a one-way traffic and the result was a vast flow of gold and silver bullion to the 'Celestial Empire'. Clocks were one of the few items which were constantly in demand in China and it is not surprising that during the eighteenth century a particular type of clock evolved which was especially made for the Chinese market.

In 1769 Father Mathieu de Benton wrote 'I have been appointed by the Emperor as clock-maker but I should rather say that I am here as machinist because the Emperor expects me to produce not really clocks but curious machines and automata'. Another contemporary writer commented that 'one should bring to Peking especially those play things which European boys use to amuse themselves. Such objects will be received here with much greater interest than scientific instruments'. The kind of toys to which he referred were probably such things as glass bottles containing little wooden mills worked by the falling of sand, rather like a sand glass. Such toys could be bought for a penny or so in Europe.

Clocks with enamelled dials which showed off to great advantage the movement of a central seconds-hand were very popular in China, as were clocks with any form of automata or musical movement. In order to avoid damage to the enamel dial or the central seconds-hand the winding squares were normally made to protrude through the back plate. Often a revolving stand was provided to facilitate turning the clock when it required winding. As well as wooden-cased clocks, gilt metal ones were frequently made for China. Often parts of the case were enamelled and decorated with split pearls and paste brilliants. In 1788 the order books of Thwaites of Clerkenwell include, for Barraud of Cornhill, 'For the China Markett. A pair of small four tune clocks with seconds in the centre, the Chime Barrill in the heade with 3 in. enamelled plates and gold hands and with a Ballance instead of Pendulums fitted into enamelled cases'. A large order follows in 1790 for '6 Pair of Plain Spring Clocks. 3 Pair of them to convex glasses and 3 to wind up behind and made in every respect suitable to the East India Trade'.

In the late eighteenth century the Chinese began to produce clocks of their own which were copies of European models. The quality of many of them is inferior to the European ones of a similar nature and it would appear that they were seldom as complicated. However, in 1800, J. Barrow was able to report that the Chinese 'now fabricate in Canton, as well as in London and at a third of the expense all those ingenious pieces of mechanism which at one time were sent to China in such quantities from the repositories of Coxe and Merlin'. This suggests that there was by this time a noticeable reduction in the import of clocks from Europe. Clocks made in China often bear on the back plate, a signature intended to be a copy of an English or Austrian name. Because the engraver did not understand European writing, he produced a quite unintelligible result.

Plate 80 – A fine quality drum-shaped table clock of brass. The case is signed on the base from where it is wound. The sides are decorated with a cast and pierced design which incorporates the Pa Chi-Hsiang or eight Buddhist symbols of the vase, the conch shell, the state umbrella, the canopy, the lotus, the flaming wheel of the law, the fish and the endless knot. The dial, which is of about 6 inches in diameter, is fitted with a single hand and points to an outer enamelled ring which displays the twelve signs of the Chinese hours. The inner ring shows the twenty-four hours of European time. The spring-driven movement uses a fusée and is controlled by a balance wheel and verge escapement. The clock also has an alarm mechanism.

Glossary

Arbor A shaft or spindle

Balance The balance, in the form of a wheel, controls the going of a clock or watch

Balance staff The arbor on which the balance is mounted

Bezel A ring, usually of brass, which surrounds the dial and is used to hold the glass

Chapters The hour numerals on a dial

Cock Bracket or bridge screwed to a clock plate in which an arbor is pivoted

Collet Brass collar used to fit a wheel to its arbor

Contrate or Bevelled wheel Wheel with its teeth cut at right angles to the plane of the wheel and used to transmit motion through 90°

Dead beat A dead beat escapement is one where no recoil is imparted to the escape wheel

Detent Locking device

Ebauche Unfinished or 'rough' movement

Escapement Link between the going train and the pendulum or balance. It is through the escapement that the impulse is given to the pendulum or balance

Fly Fan-like governor used to regulate the speed of the striking train

Foliot Bar balance used with the verge escapement in early clocks

Fusée See p. 11

Gathering pallet A single-leafed pinion, used in rack striking, which gathers the teeth of the rack, one at a time

Going barrel Mainspring barrel which incorporates the great wheel.

The motion is transmitted directly from the spring to the great wheel without using a fusée

Going train That train of wheels from which the hands are drived

Impulse face Any part of an escapement which receives an impulse from the escape wheel

Lantern pinion Pinion, with pins, held between two metal disks, which act as the leaves or teeth

Motion work The wheels and pinions, mounted behind the dial, which drive the hands of a clock, normally giving a 12:1 reduction ratio

Pallet The parts of an escapement upon which the escape wheel acts. On some escapements one part may be locking and another for receiving an impulse

Pinion A wheel with few teeth. The teeth, or leaves, are normally cut from the same piece of metal as its arbor

Recoil A recoil escapement is one where the escape wheel is made to recoil by the pallets

Set-up The amount by which a spring remains wound when the clock is run down

Train A number of wheels and pinions geared to one another

Bibliography

Basserman, Jordan, *The Book of Old Clocks and Watches* (Allen & Unwin, 1964)

Battison, Edwin A. and Kane, Patricia E., *The American Clock 1725–1865*. Greenwich, Conn: New York Graphic Society, Ltd., 1973.

Britten, F. J., *Watch & Clockmakers Handbook* (E. & F. N. Spon, 1946)

Cescinsky and Webster, *English Domestic Clocks* (Hamlyn, 1969)

Drummond, Robertson, *The Evolution of Clockwork* (S.R. Publishers Ltd., 1931)

Edey, Winthrop, *French Clocks* (Studio Vista, 1967)

Hoopes, Penrose R., *Connecticut Clockmakers of the Eighteenth Century*. Hartford, E. V. Mitchell, 1930 (Reprinted 1974 by Dover Books)

Jerome, Chauncey, *History of the American Clock Business for the past Sixty Years*. New Haven: F. C. Dayton, 1860 (Reprinted by Adams Brown Co., Exeter, N.H.)

Lloyd, H. Alan, *The Collector's Dictionary of Clocks* (Country Life, 1964)

Palmer, Brooks, *The Book of American Clocks* (Macmillan, 1972)

Roberts, Kenneth D., *The Contributions of Joseph Ives to Connecticut Clock Technology*, 1810–1862. Bristol, Conn.: The American Clock & Watch Museum, 1970.

Roberts, Kenneth D., *Eli Terry and the Connecticut Shelf Clock*. Bristol, Conn.: Ken Roberts Publishing Co., 1973.

Symonds, R. W., *A Book of English Clocks* (Penguin, 1947)

Tyler, E. J., *European Clocks* (Ward Lock, 1968)

Ward, F. A. B., *Time Measurement* (H.M.S.O., 1966)

Acknowledgments

The author and publishers wish to thank the following for allowing the reproduction of the illustrations in this book:

Mr M. Aalders, 13b; the American Clock and Watch Museum, Bristol, Conn., U.S.A., 67–70 (photographed by Edward Goodrich); the Antique Porcelain Co., London, 31, 53; the British Museum, London, 4, 71 (photos by courtesy of Weidenfeld and Nicolson); Aubrey Brocklehurst Antique Clocks, London, 6, 10, 11b; Adrian Burchall, Antique Clocks, Bristol, 12c, 55, 63, 65; Mrs S. Burchall, 36; Camerer Cuss & Co., London, 3b, 11a, 39, 46; the Clock Clinic, London, 21, 22, 34a; the Clockmakers Company Museum, London, 3a (photo by courtesy of Weidenfeld and Nicolson); Mr G Eadington, 72c; Bartholomew Flaggett Antiques, London, 38, 66, 72a, 72b; the Holburne of Menstrie Museum, Bath, 32, 48a, 51; Johann Klein Antique Clocks, London, 8, 23b, 24, 45a, 60a; Malletts, London, 54; the Netherlands Gold, Silver and Clock Museum, Utrecht, 9, 18, 19, 35 (Museum photographs); Perio Antiques, London, 12a, 12b, 13a, 13c, 40a, 40b, 73, 74b, 74c; the Science Museum, London, 1, 2, 15, 16, 20, 43, 44, 75b, 76, 78b, 79, and plates 75c, 77, 78a, 80 (from the collection of the late P. L. Harrison, Esq.); Mrs J. Simpson, 59a; Strike One Ltd, London, 34b, 52; the Victoria and Albert Museum, London, 5, 17 (Museum photo), 23a, 25, 26, 28, 29, 30, 45b, 48b, 50; the Wallace Collection, London, 27, 33 (Museum photographs); Mr R. C. Woofinden, 42; Mr J. Woollard, 47.

All photographs by Bob Loosemore, except where otherwise stated.

Clock and Watch Collections

ENGLAND

Bury St Edmunds Gershom-Parkington Memorial Collection of Time Measurement Instruments, Angel Corner, Bury St Edmunds

Cambridge Fitzwilliam Museum, Trumpington St., Cambridge CB2 1RB

Lincoln Usher Gallery, Lindum Rd., Lincoln

Liverpool City of Liverpool Museum, William Brown St., Liverpool L3 8EN

London British Museum, Great Russell St., WC1B 3DG
Clockmakers' Company Museum, the Guildhall, EC2
National Maritime Museum, Greenwich, SE10
Science Museum, Exhibition Rd., South Kensington, SW7
Victoria and Albert Museum, South Kensington, SW7

Oxford Ashmolean Museum of Art and Archaeology, Beaumont St., Oxford
Museum of the History of Science, Broad St., Oxford OX1 3AZ

AUSTRIA

Vienna Clock Museum
Kunsthistorisches Museum

DENMARK

Aarhus Danish Urmuseum

Copenhagen National Museum
Rosenborg Castle Museum

FRANCE
Besancon Musée des Beaux Arts
Paris Conservatoire des Arts et Métiers
Louvre
Musée des Arts Decoratifs
Toulouse Musée Paul Dupuy
Musée Saint Raymond

GERMANY
Augsburg City Museum
Baden Wurttemberg Collection Landesgewerbeamt
Furtwangen Clock Museum
Munich Bavarian National Museum
Nuremburg Germanisches National Museum
Schwenningen Collections of the Mauthe & Kienzle Factories

HOLLAND
Amsterdam Rijksmuseum
Groningen Groningen Museum
Leiden Dutch Science Museum
Utrecht Netherlands Gold, Silver and Clock Museum

SWEDEN
Stockholm Nordliches Museum
Stadsmuseum

SWITZERLAND
Basel Kirchgarten Museum
Geneva Musée d'Horologerie
La Chaux de Fonds Musée d'Horologerie
Le Locle Musée d'Horologerie
Neuchatel Musée Historique

U.S.A.

CALIFORNIA
San Francisco California Academy of Sciences, Golden Gate Park, San Francisco, 94118

COLORADO
Denver Hagans Clock Manor Museum, Bergen Park, Evergreen, Denver, 80439

CONNECTICUT
Bristol American Clock and Watch Museum, Inc, 100 Maple St., Bristol, 06010

ILLINOIS
Chicago Adler Planetarium and Astronomical Museum, 1300 S. Lakeshore Drive, Chicago, 60605
Springfield Illinois State Museum, Spring & Edwards Sts., Springfield, 62706

MASSACHUSETTS
Sturbridge Old Sturbridge Village, Sturbridge, 01566

NEW YORK
New York James Arthur Collection, New York University, Washington Square Metropolitan Museum of Art, Fifth Ave. at 82nd St., 10028

OHIO
Cincinnati Taft Museum, 316 Pike St., 45202

PENNSYLVANIA
Columbia National Association of Watch and Clock Collectors, 514 Poplar St., 17512

VERMONT
Shelburne Shelburne Museum, Shelburne, 05482

WASHINGTON D.C. Smithsonian Institution, 1000 Jefferson Drive S.W., 20560

Index